Mastering IT Solutions Architecture

Architecture

A Comprehensive Guide for

Beginners and Practitioners

By: Olu Ogunsakin

Contents

Chapter 1: Introduction to IT Solutions Architecture

1.1. Understanding the Role of an IT Solutions Architect

An IT Solutions Architect is a pivotal figure in the design, development, and implementation of IT systems within an organisation. They act as a bridge between business stakeholders and technical teams, translating complex business requirements into scalable, secure, and efficient technical solutions. Their role encompasses analysing existing systems, identifying gaps, and proposing innovative solutions that align with the organisation's strategic objectives.

1.2. Key Responsibilities of an IT Solutions Architect

1.2.1. Requirement Analysis

a. Collaborating with stakeholders to understand business needs and technical constraints.

b. Conducting workshops and interviews to gather detailed requirements.

c. Documenting functional and non-functional requirements (e.g., scalability, security, performance).

1.2.2. System Design

a. Creating blueprints for IT systems that integrate seamlessly with existing infrastructure.

b. Designing modular, reusable, and maintainable components.

c. Ensuring the architecture aligns with industry best practices and standards.

1.2.3. Technology Evaluation:

a. Assessing and selecting the right tools, platforms, and frameworks to meet business goals.

b. Comparing technologies based on cost, scalability, and compatibility with existing systems.

c. Staying updated on emerging technologies (e.g., AI, IoT, blockchain) and their potential applications.

1.2.4. Stakeholder Communication

a. Presenting technical solutions in a clear, non-technical manner to business leaders.

b. Creating visual representations (e.g., diagrams, flowcharts) to explain complex concepts.

c. Managing expectations and ensuring alignment between business and technical teams.

1.2.5. Implementation Oversight

a. Guiding development teams to ensure the solution is built as designed.

b. Conducting regular reviews to ensure adherence to architectural principles.

c. Troubleshooting issues and providing technical guidance during the implementation phase.

Real-Life Example

Consider a large e-commerce company planning to revamp its online platform to improve user experience and boost sales. The IT Solutions Architect would:

- Conduct a thorough assessment of the current system architecture, identifying bottlenecks and areas for improvement.

- Gather requirements from stakeholders, including marketing, sales, and IT teams, to understand their needs and pain points.
- Design a new architecture that supports scalability (to handle peak traffic during sales events), security (to protect customer data), and performance (to ensure fast page load times).
- Present the proposed architecture to senior management, using visual aids to explain the benefits and ROI.
- Oversee the implementation, ensuring the development team adheres to the design and addressing any technical challenges that arise.

This holistic approach ensures the new platform not only meets immediate business needs but is also future-proofed for growth.

1.3. Importance of IT Solutions Architecture in Modern Organisations

In today's fast-paced digital landscape, organisations rely heavily on technology to remain competitive, drive innovation, and deliver value to customers. IT Solutions Architecture plays a critical role in ensuring that technology investments align with business goals and deliver measurable outcomes. By designing robust and efficient IT

systems, Solutions Architects help organisations streamline
processes, reduce costs, and stay ahead of the competition.

1.3.1. Why IT Solutions Architecture Matters

1.3.1.1. Alignment with Business Goals
   a. Ensures IT initiatives support the organisation's strategic
       objectives.
   b. Bridges the gap between business and technology, enabling
       better decision-making.

1.3.1.2. Cost Efficiency
   a. Reduces wasted resources by designing systems that are
       scalable and maintainable.
   b. Minimises technical debt by avoiding short-term fixes and
       ensuring long-term sustainability.

1.3.1.3. Risk Mitigation:
   a. Identifies potential risks early in the design phase and
       proposes mitigation strategies.
   b. Ensures compliance with regulatory requirements (e.g.,
       GDPR, HIPAA).

1.3.1.4.   Innovation Enablement

a. Provides a foundation for adopting emerging technologies like AI, IoT, and cloud computing.

b. Encourages experimentation and innovation by creating flexible, modular architectures.

1.3.2. Real-Life Example

A multinational corporation with disparate IT systems across its business units faced challenges in collaboration and data sharing. An IT Solutions Architect was brought in to develop an integrated architecture. The solution:

- Unified data storage and access across departments, enabling seamless communication and collaboration.
- Improved productivity by reducing duplication of efforts and streamlining workflows.
- Reduced IT overhead costs by consolidating redundant systems and optimising resource usage.

The result was a 20% increase in operational efficiency and a significant reduction in IT overhead costs.

1.4. <u>Career Path and Opportunities for IT Solutions Architects</u>

Becoming an IT Solutions Architect offers a rewarding and dynamic career path with abundant opportunities for growth and advancement. This role is ideal for individuals who enjoy solving complex problems, working at the intersection of business and technology, and driving impactful change within organisations.

1.4.1. Typical Career Progression

1.4.1.1. Entry-Level Roles:

a. Business Analyst: Gains experience in understanding business requirements and translating them into technical solutions.
b. Data Analyst: Develops expertise in data analysis and visualisation, laying the groundwork for system design.
c. Software Developer: Builds technical skills in programming and software development, essential for understanding system architecture.

1.4.1.2.   Mid-Level Roles

a. Systems Analyst: Focuses on analysing and improving existing systems, gaining experience in system design and project management.

b. Technical Lead: Leads development teams, gaining experience in guiding technical projects and mentoring junior team members.

1.4.1.3.   Senior Roles

a. IT Solutions Architect: Leads architecture initiatives, designing and implementing complex IT systems.

b. Enterprise Architect: Guides the organisation's overall technology strategy, ensuring alignment with business goals.

1.4.2. Skills and Certifications

- Technical Skills: Proficiency in cloud platforms (AWS, Azure), programming languages (Python, Java), and architecture frameworks (TOGAF, Zachman).

- Soft Skills: Strong communication, problem-solving, and stakeholder management abilities.

- Certifications: TOGAF, AWS Certified Solutions Architect, or Microsoft Certified: Azure Solutions Architect.

1.4.2.1. Real-Life Example

John, a Business Analyst with a background in software development, transitioned to the role of an IT Solutions Architect after gaining experience on various projects within his organisation. He pursued additional training and certifications, including TOGAF and AWS Certified Solutions Architect, to enhance his architectural skills. Over time, John became a trusted advisor to senior management, guiding the organisation's technology strategy and leading high-impact projects.

1.5. Interactive Features and Exercises

To help readers engage with the content and apply the concepts, this chapter includes the following interactive elements:

1.5.1. Scenario-Based Exercise

a. Scenario: You are an IT Solutions Architect for a retail company planning to launch a new mobile app. The app must integrate with the existing e-commerce platform and support features like personalised recommendations and secure payments.

b. Task: Outline the key steps you would take to design the solution architecture. Consider scalability, security, and user experience.

1.5.2. Reflection Prompt

a. Question: Think about a project you've worked on or observed. What were the architectural challenges, and how could they have been addressed?

1.5.3. Checklist for Aspiring Solutions Architects

a. Understand the organisation's business goals and technical constraints.

b. Develop a strong foundation in system design and architecture frameworks.

c. Build communication and stakeholder management skills.

d. Pursue relevant certifications to enhance your expertise.

1.5.4. Real-World Examples

To provide deeper context, this chapter includes additional examples from various industries:

1.5.4.1. Healthcare

A hospital needed a new patient management system to handle increasing patient loads and comply with data privacy regulations. The IT Solutions Architect designed a cloud-based solution that improved data accessibility for healthcare providers while ensuring compliance with GDPR and HIPAA.

1.5.4.2.   Retail

A fashion retailer wanted to enhance its online shopping experience. The Solutions Architect proposed a microservices-based architecture that allowed for rapid deployment of new features, such as virtual try-ons and AI-driven product recommendations.

1.5.4.3.   Hospitality

A hotel chain sought to integrate its booking, customer service, and loyalty programs into a single platform. The Solutions Architect designed an architecture that streamlined operations and provided a seamless experience for guests.

1.6.   Conclusion

IT Solutions Architecture is a cornerstone of modern organisations, enabling them to harness technology for strategic advantage. Whether you're just starting your journey or looking to deepen your expertise, this chapter has laid the foundation for understanding the role, importance, and career opportunities in this field. As you progress through this book, you'll gain the knowledge and tools needed to excel as an IT Solutions Architect.

Additional Resources

a. The Open Group - IT Architecture Certification Programs: Certifications | www.opengroup.org

b. Microsoft Learn - Azure Solutions Architect Training: Microsoft Certified: Azure Solutions Architect Expert - Certifications | Microsoft Learn

c. IBM Developer - Cloud Architecture Center: IBM Cloud Architecture Center - IBM MediaCenter

Chapter 2: Fundamentals of IT Architecture

2.1. Introduction to IT Solutions Architecture Fundamentals

IT Solutions Architecture is the backbone of any successful IT system, ensuring that technology aligns with business goals and delivers measurable value. This chapter will guide you through the foundational principles, methodologies, and frameworks that underpin effective solution architecture. Whether you're a beginner or a seasoned practitioner, this chapter will provide the tools and insights needed to design robust, scalable, and efficient IT systems.

2.2. Core Principles of IT Solutions Architecture

Understanding the core principles of IT Solutions Architecture is essential for designing systems that meet business needs while remaining flexible and future-proof. These principles serve as the foundation for all architectural decisions and ensure consistency across projects.

2.2.1. Key Principles

2.2.1.1. Modularity

a. Designing systems as independent, reusable components.

b. Example: A retail company uses a modular architecture to separate its inventory management system from its payment gateway, allowing each component to be updated independently.

2.2.1.2. Scalability

a. Ensuring systems can handle increased loads without performance degradation.

b. Example: A streaming service uses cloud-based auto-scaling to accommodate millions of users during peak hours.

2.2.1.3. Security

a. Protecting systems from unauthorised access and data breaches.

b. Example: A healthcare provider implements encryption and multi-factor authentication to secure patient data.

2.2.1.4. Performance

a. Optimising systems for speed and efficiency.

b. Example: An e-commerce platform uses caching and content delivery networks (CDNs) to reduce page load times.

2.2.1.5. *Maintainability*

a. Designing systems that are easy to update and troubleshoot.

b. Example: A financial institution adopts microservices architecture to simplify maintenance and reduce downtime.

2.2.2. Real-Life Example

A global logistics company faced challenges with its legacy system, which was slow, difficult to maintain, and unable to scale. An IT Solutions Architect redesigned the system using modular, scalable, and secure principles. The new architecture reduced downtime by 30% and improved system performance by 50%.

2.3. Methodologies and Frameworks for IT Solutions Architecture

To design effective IT systems, Solutions Architects rely on proven methodologies and frameworks. These tools provide a structured approach to architecture design and ensure alignment with industry best practices.

2.3.1. Popular Methodologies and Frameworks

2.3.1.1.   TOGAF (The Open Group Architecture Framework)
a. A comprehensive framework for enterprise architecture.
b. Example: A manufacturing company uses TOGAF to align its IT systems with business goals, resulting in a 20% increase in operational efficiency.

2.3.1.2.   Zachman Framework
a. A taxonomy for organising architectural artefacts.
b. Example: A government agency uses the Zachman Framework to document its IT systems, improving transparency and accountability.

2.3.1.3.   Agile Architecture:
a. An iterative approach to architecture design.
b. Example: A software development firm adopts Agile Architecture to deliver incremental updates to its product, reducing time-to-market by 40%.

2.3.1.4.   Microservices Architecture:
a. Designing systems as a collection of small, independent services.

b. Example: A retail giant uses microservices to enable rapid deployment of new features, such as personalised recommendations and real-time inventory updates.

2.3.2. Real-Life Example

A telecommunications company struggled with its monolithic architecture, which was slow to adapt to changing market demands. By adopting microservices architecture, the company reduced deployment times from weeks to hours and improved customer satisfaction by 25%.

2.4. Industry-Specific Applications of IT Solutions Architecture

IT Solutions Architecture is not a one-size-fits-all discipline. Different industries have unique requirements and challenges, necessitating tailored approaches to architecture design.

2.4.1. Industry-Specific Examples

2.4.1.1. Healthcare

a. Challenge: A hospital needed a patient management system that could handle increasing patient loads while complying with data privacy regulations.

b. Solution: The IT Solutions Architect designed a cloud-based system with encryption and access controls, ensuring compliance with GDPR and HIPAA.
c. Outcome: The new system improved data accessibility for healthcare providers and reduced administrative overhead by 15%.

2.4.1.2. Retail

a. Challenge: A fashion retailer wanted to enhance its online shopping experience to compete with e-commerce giants.
b. Solution: The Solutions Architect proposed a microservices-based architecture, enabling rapid deployment of features like virtual try-ons and AI-driven product recommendations.
c. Outcome: The retailer saw a 30% increase in online sales and a 20% improvement in customer satisfaction.

2.4.1.3. Hospitality:

a. Challenge: A hotel chain sought to integrate its booking, customer service, and loyalty programs into a single platform.
b. Solution: The Solutions Architect designed an integrated architecture that streamlined operations and provided a seamless experience for guests.
c. Outcome: The hotel chain achieved a 25% increase in bookings and a 15% reduction in operational costs.

Chapter 2

2.4.2. Interactive Features and Exercises

To help readers engage with the content and apply the concepts, this chapter includes the following interactive elements:

2.4.2.1.   Scenario-Based Exercise

a. Scenario: You are an IT Solutions Architect for a healthcare provider planning to implement a telemedicine platform. The platform must support video consultations, patient data storage, and integration with existing systems.
b. Task: Outline the key steps you would take to design the solution architecture. Consider scalability, security, and compliance with data privacy regulations.

2.4.2.2.   Reflection Prompt

a. Question: Think about a system you've used or observed. How does it align with the core principles of IT Solutions Architecture? What improvements would you suggest?

2.4.2.3.   Checklist for Designing Effective Architectures:

a. Understand the organisation's business goals and technical constraints.
b. Choose the right methodology or framework for the project.
c. Design for modularity, scalability, security, performance, and maintainability.
d. Test the architecture with real-world scenarios and iterate as needed.

2.4.3. Real-World Case Studies

To provide deeper context, this chapter includes additional case studies from various industries:

2.4.3.1. Finance

A bank needed to modernise its legacy systems to improve customer experience and reduce costs. The IT Solutions Architect designed a cloud-based architecture that enabled real-time transactions and reduced infrastructure costs by 30%.

2.4.3.2. Education

A university wanted to create a unified platform for online learning, student management, and administrative tasks. The Solutions Architect proposed a modular architecture that integrated existing systems and provided a seamless experience for students and staff.

2.4.3.3. Manufacturing

A car manufacturer sought to implement an IoT-based system for predictive maintenance. The Solutions Architect designed a scalable architecture that collected data from sensors and used machine learning to predict equipment failures, reducing downtime by 20%.

2.5. <u>Conclusion</u>

The fundamentals of IT Solutions Architecture provide the foundation for designing systems that meet business needs and deliver measurable value. By understanding the core principles, methodologies, and industry-specific applications, you can create architectures that are robust, scalable, and future-proof. As you progress through this book, you'll gain the knowledge and tools needed to excel as an IT Solutions Architect.

<u>Additional Resources</u>

- The Open Group - TOGAF Certification and Training: <u>TOGAF® 9 Certification | www.opengroup.org</u>

- Zachman International - Enterprise Architecture Certification: <u>Home - Zachman International - FEAC Institute (zachman-feac.com)</u>

- <u>Microsoft Learn - Cloud Architecture Learning Path:</u> <u>Azure on Microsoft Learn | Microsoft Learn</u>

- <u>Amazon Web Services (AWS) Training and Certification:</u> <u>AWS training and certification</u>

- <u>Google Cloud - Architecting with Google Cloud Training:</u> <u>Professional Cloud Architect Certification | Learn | Google Cloud</u>

Chapter 3: Designing Effective IT Solutions – From Requirements to Implementation

3.1. Introduction to Designing IT Solutions

Designing effective IT solutions is a multi-step process that begins with understanding business requirements and ends with successful implementation. This chapter will guide you through each stage of the design process, providing practical tools, techniques, and real-world examples to help you create solutions that deliver value to your organisation.

3.2. Understanding Business Requirements

The foundation of any successful IT solution is a clear understanding of business requirements. This stage involves collaborating with stakeholders to identify their needs, goals, and pain points.

3.2.1. Key Steps

3.2.1.1. Stakeholder Engagement

a. Conduct workshops, interviews, and surveys to gather input from key stakeholders.

b. Example: A retail company engages store managers, sales teams, and IT staff to identify requirements for a new point-of-sale (POS) system.

3.2.1.2. Requirement Documentation

a. Document functional requirements (what the system should do) and non-functional requirements (how the system should perform).

b. Example: A healthcare provider documents requirements for a telemedicine platform, including video call functionality, patient data storage, and compliance with GDPR.

3.2.1.3. Prioritisation

a. Use techniques like MoSCoW (Must have, Should have, Could have, Won't have) to prioritise requirements.

b. Example: A logistics company prioritises real-time tracking (Must have) over advanced analytics (Could have) for its fleet management system.

3.2.2. Real-Life Example

A financial institution wanted to modernise its legacy banking system. The IT Solutions Architect conducted stakeholder workshops and identified key requirements, including real-time transaction processing, fraud detection, and mobile banking capabilities. By prioritising these requirements, the team was able to focus on delivering the most critical features first.

3.3.   Translating Requirements into Technical Specifications

Once business requirements are understood, the next step is to translate them into technical specifications. This involves designing the system architecture, selecting technologies, and defining interfaces.

3.3.1. Key Steps

3.3.1.1.   System Design

a. Create high-level and low-level designs, including architecture diagrams, data flow diagrams, and interface specifications.

b. Example: A retail company designs a microservices-based architecture for its e-commerce platform, with separate services for product catalogues, shopping carts, and payments.

3.3.1.2. Technology Selection

a. Evaluate and select technologies based on factors like scalability, security, and cost.

b. Example: A healthcare provider chooses AWS for its telemedicine platform due to its scalability and compliance with data privacy regulations.

3.3.1.3. Prototyping

a. Build prototypes to validate design decisions and gather feedback from stakeholders.

b. Example: A logistics company creates a prototype of its real-time tracking system to demonstrate functionality to stakeholders.

3.3.2. Real-Life Example

A telecommunications company needed to design a new billing system. The IT Solutions Architect created a high-level design using TOGAF, selected a cloud-based platform for scalability, and built a prototype to validate the design. The final system reduced billing errors by 20% and improved customer satisfaction.

3.4. Implementation and Deployment

The implementation phase involves building, testing, and deploying the solution. This stage requires close collaboration between the Solutions Architect, development teams, and stakeholders.

3.4.1. Key Steps

3.4.1.1. Development

a. Guide development teams to ensure the solution is built according to the design.

b. Example: A retail company uses Agile methodology to develop its e-commerce platform, with regular sprints and reviews.

3.4.1.2. Testing

a. Conduct unit testing, integration testing, and user acceptance testing (UAT) to ensure the solution meets requirements.

b. Example: A healthcare provider tests its telemedicine platform with real users to identify and fix issues before launch.

3.4.1.3.   Deployment

a. Deploy the solution in a controlled manner, using techniques like blue-green deployment or canary releases.

b. Example: A logistics company uses blue-green deployment to minimise downtime during the rollout of its real-time tracking system.

3.4.2. Real-Life Example

A financial institution implemented a new mobile banking app. The IT Solutions Architect guided the development team, conducted rigorous testing, and used a phased deployment strategy to ensure a smooth rollout. The app received positive feedback from users and increased mobile transactions by 30%.

3.5. <u>Post-Implementation Review and Optimisation</u>

After deployment, it's important to review the solution's performance and make optimisations as needed.

3.5.1. Key Steps

3.5.1.1.   *Performance Monitoring:*
  a. Use monitoring tools to track system performance and identify bottlenecks.
  b. Example: A retail company uses AWS CloudWatch to monitor its e-commerce platform and optimise server performance.

3.5.1.2.   *User Feedback:*
  a. Gather feedback from users to identify areas for improvement.
  b. Example: A healthcare provider conducts surveys with patients and doctors to improve its telemedicine platform.

3.5.1.3.   *Continuous Improvement:*
  a. Implement changes based on feedback and performance data.
  b. Example: A logistics company uses A/B testing to optimise its real-time tracking system's user interface.

3.5.2. Real-Life Example

A telecommunications company conducted a post-implementation review of its billing system and identified opportunities to improve performance. By optimising database queries and adding caching, the company reduced response times by 40%.

3.6. Interactive Features and Exercises

To help readers engage with the content and apply the concepts, this chapter includes the following interactive elements:

3.6.1.1. Scenario-Based Exercise

a. Scenario: You are an IT Solutions Architect for a retail company planning to launch a new mobile app. The app must integrate with the existing e-commerce platform and support features like personalised recommendations and secure payments.

b. Task: Outline the key steps you would take to design and implement the solution. Consider scalability, security, and user experience.

3.6.1.2. Reflection Prompt

a. Question: Think about a project you've worked on or observed. What were the key challenges during the design and implementation phases, and how could they have been addressed?

3.6.1.3.   Checklist for Designing and Implementing IT Solutions:
   a.   Understand and document business requirements.
   b.   Translate requirements into technical specifications.
   b.   Guide development and testing teams.
   c.   Deploy the solution and conduct post-implementation reviews.

3.6.2. Real-World Case Studies

To provide deeper context, this chapter includes additional case studies from various industries:

3.6.2.1.   Finance

A bank needed to modernise its legacy systems to improve customer experience and reduce costs. The IT Solutions Architect designed a cloud-based architecture that enabled real-time transactions and reduced infrastructure costs by 30%.

3.6.2.2.   Education

A university wanted to create a unified platform for online learning, student management, and administrative tasks. The

Solutions Architect proposed a modular architecture that integrated existing systems and provided a seamless experience for students and staff.

3.6.2.3. *Manufacturing*

A car manufacturer sought to implement an IoT-based system for predictive maintenance. The Solutions Architect designed a scalable architecture that collected data from sensors and used machine learning to predict equipment failures, reducing downtime by 20%.

3.7. Conclusion

Designing effective IT solutions requires a structured approach, from understanding business requirements to successful implementation. By following the steps outlined in this chapter, you can create solutions that deliver value to your organisation and meet the needs of your stakeholders. As you progress through this book, you'll gain the knowledge and tools needed to excel as an IT Solutions Architect.

Additional Resources

- AWS Training and Certification: AWS Certification | AWS Training & Certification

- Microsoft Learn - Azure Fundamentals: Microsoft Certified: Azure Fundamentals - Certifications | Microsoft Learn

- Google Cloud Training: Google Cloud Courses and Training | Google Cloud

- **VMware Hands-on Labs:** VMware Discovery by Hands-on Labs

- **Docker Documentation:** Docker Docs

- **Kubernetes Documentation:** Kubernetes Documentation | Kubernetes

- MongoDB University: MongoDB

- Apache Spark Documentation: Documentation | Apache Spark

Data Warehousing Concepts and Best Practices: What Is Data Warehousing? Concepts, Best Practices, and Tools | Airbyte; Data Warehouse Best Practices and Concepts: 8 Steps How To Build a Data Warehouse (dataart.com)

Chapter 4: Technical Skills for IT Solutions Architects

4.1. Introduction to Technical Skills for IT Solutions Architects

IT Solutions Architects must possess a diverse set of technical skills to design, implement, and manage complex IT systems. This chapter explores the key technical competencies required, including system design, cloud computing, networking, and data management. By mastering these skills, Solutions Architects can create robust, scalable, and secure solutions that meet business needs.

4.2. Proficiency in System Design and Integration

System design and integration are at the core of an IT Solutions Architect's role. These skills enable the creation of scalable, reliable, and secure IT solutions that align with business objectives.

4.2.1. Key Areas of Focus

4.2.1.1. System Design Principles

a. Understanding design patterns (e.g., MVC, microservices) and architectural styles (e.g., monolithic, layered).

b. Best practices for designing robust and maintainable systems, such as modularity and loose coupling.

c. Example: A retail company uses a layered architecture to separate its user interface, business logic, and data access layers, improving maintainability.

4.2.1.2. Integration Technologies

a. Familiarity with APIs (REST, GraphQL), messaging queues (Kafka, RabbitMQ), and ETL (Extract, Transform, Load) processes.

b. Example: A logistics company uses APIs to integrate its tracking system with third-party delivery services, enabling real-time updates.

4.2.1.3. Enterprise Application Integration (EAI):

a. Knowledge of EAI techniques and tools (e.g., MuleSoft, Dell Boomi) for integrating disparate applications and data sources.

    b. Example: A healthcare provider uses EAI to integrate its electronic health record (EHR) system with billing and scheduling applications.

4.2.1.4. Microservices Architecture:

    a. Understanding the principles of microservices architecture and its advantages in building modular and loosely coupled systems.

    b. Example: A financial institution adopts microservices to enable independent deployment of its payment processing and fraud detection modules.

4.2.2. Real-Life Example

A retail company revamped its e-commerce platform by adopting a microservices architecture. By decomposing its monolithic application into independently deployable services, the organisation achieved greater agility, scalability, and fault isolation. For instance, the product catalogue service could be updated without affecting the shopping cart or payment services.

4.3. <u>Knowledge of Cloud Computing Technologies</u>

Cloud computing has revolutionised IT infrastructure, offering scalability, flexibility, and cost-efficiency. IT Solutions Architects must be well-versed in cloud technologies to design modern solutions.

4.3.1. Key Areas of Knowledge

4.3.1.1.   Cloud Service Models:

a. Understanding the differences between Infrastructure as a Service (IaaS), Platform as a Service (PaaS), Integration Platform as a Service (iPaaS), and Software as a Service (SaaS).

b. Example: A startup uses SaaS for its CRM system, PaaS for application development, and IaaS for hosting its website.

4.3.1.2.   Cloud Providers

a. Familiarity with major cloud service providers such as Amazon Web Services (AWS), Microsoft Azure, and Google Cloud Platform (GCP).

b. Example: A media company uses AWS for its video streaming platform due to its global content delivery network (CDN) and scalability.

4.3.1.3.   Cloud Architecture Patterns:

a. Knowledge of patterns such as serverless computing, containerisation, and hybrid cloud deployment strategies.

b. Example: A logistics company uses serverless computing for its real-time tracking system, reducing infrastructure management overhead.

4.3.1.4.   Security and Compliance:

a. Understanding cloud security best practices, compliance requirements (e.g., GDPR, HIPAA), and tools for securing cloud-based applications and data.

b. Example: A healthcare provider uses Azure's built-in compliance features to ensure its telemedicine platform meets regulatory requirements.

4.3.2. Real-Life Example

A financial services company migrated its legacy on-premises infrastructure to the cloud to improve scalability and reduce operational costs. By leveraging AWS's serverless computing capabilities, the organisation achieved greater agility and cost savings while maintaining compliance with industry regulations.

4.4. Understanding of Networking and Infrastructure

Networking and infrastructure form the backbone of IT systems, providing connectivity and support for applications and services.

4.4.1. Key Areas of Understanding

4.4.1.1. Network Protocols and Technologies

a. Familiarity with TCP/IP, DNS, DHCP, VPN, and other networking protocols and technologies.

b. Example: A retail company uses VPNs to securely connect its remote stores to the central inventory management system.

4.4.1.2. Network Design and Architecture

a. Knowledge of network design principles, including segmentation, redundancy, and fault tolerance.

b. Example: A financial institution designs a redundant network architecture to ensure high availability for its online banking platform.

4.4.1.3.   *Virtualisation and Containerisation*

a. Understanding virtualisation technologies (e.g., VMware, Hyper-V) and containerisation platforms (e.g., Docker, Kubernetes).

b. Example: A software development firm uses Kubernetes to orchestrate containerised applications, improving deployment efficiency.

4.4.1.4.   *Software-Defined Networking (SDN):*

a. Awareness of SDN concepts and technologies for programmable, automated network management.

b. Example: A healthcare organisation implements SDN to dynamically adjust network configurations based on traffic patterns.

4.4.2. Real-Life Example

A healthcare organisation implemented a software-defined networking solution to improve network agility and flexibility. By abstracting network control from hardware devices and centralising management, the organisation could dynamically adjust network configurations to meet changing business needs, such as prioritising telemedicine traffic during peak hours.

4.5. Familiarity with Data Management and Database Systems

Effective data management is critical for ensuring data integrity, availability, and security.

4.5.1. Key Areas of Knowledge

4.5.1.1. Relational and NoSQL Databases

a. Understanding of relational database management systems (RDBMS) such as MySQL, PostgreSQL, and Oracle, as well as NoSQL databases like MongoDB, Cassandra, and Redis.

b. Example: An e-commerce company uses MySQL for transactional data and MongoDB for storing unstructured product reviews.

4.5.1.2. Data Modeling and Schema Design

a. Proficiency in data modelling techniques, normalisation, denormalisation, and schema design for optimising database performance and scalability.

b. Example: A logistics company designs a denormalised schema for its real-time tracking system to reduce query latency.

4.5.1.3. Big Data Technologies

a. Familiarity with big data technologies such as Hadoop, Spark, and HDFS for processing and analysing large volumes of data.

b. Example: A telecommunications company uses Spark to analyse call data records and identify network performance issues.

4.5.1.4. Data Warehousing and Business Intelligence

a. Knowledge of data warehousing concepts, ETL processes, and BI tools (e.g., Tableau, Power BI) for extracting insights from data.

b. Example: A retail company uses a data warehouse to consolidate sales data from multiple stores and generate actionable insights.

4.5.2. Real-Life Example

A telecommunications company implemented a data warehouse solution to consolidate and analyse customer data from multiple sources. By centralising data storage and implementing ETL processes, the organisation gained actionable insights into customer behaviour and preferences, enabling targeted marketing campaigns and service improvements.

4.6. Interactive Features and Exercises

To help readers engage with the content and apply the concepts, this chapter includes the following interactive elements:

4.6.1.1. *Scenario-Based Exercise*

a. Scenario: You are an IT Solutions Architect for a healthcare provider planning to implement a telemedicine platform. The platform must support video consultations, patient data storage, and integration with existing systems.

b. Task: Outline the key steps you would take to design the solution architecture. Consider scalability, security, and compliance with data privacy regulations.

4.6.1.2. *Reflection Prompt*

a. Question: Think about a system you've used or observed. How does it align with the core principles of IT Solutions Architecture? What improvements would you suggest?

4.6.1.3. *Checklist for Designing Effective Architectures*

a. Understand the organisation's business goals and technical constraints.

b. Choose the right methodology or framework for the project.

c. Design for modularity, scalability, security, performance, and maintainability.

d. Test the architecture with real-world scenarios and iterate as needed.

4.7. Real-World Case Studies

To provide deeper context, this chapter includes additional case studies from various industries:

4.7.1.1.   *Finance*

A bank needed to modernise its legacy systems to improve customer experience and reduce costs. The IT Solutions Architect designed a cloud-based architecture that enabled real-time transactions and reduced infrastructure costs by 30%.

4.7.1.2.   *Education*

A university wanted to create a unified platform for online learning, student management, and administrative tasks. The Solutions Architect proposed a modular architecture that integrated existing systems and provided a seamless experience for students and staff.

4.7.1.3.   Manufacturing:

A car manufacturer sought to implement an IoT-based system for predictive maintenance. The Solutions Architect designed a scalable architecture that collected data from sensors and used machine learning to predict equipment failures, reducing downtime by 20%.

4.8. Conclusion

The technical skills outlined in this chapter are essential for IT Solutions Architects to design, implement, and manage effective IT solutions. By mastering system design, cloud computing, networking, and data management, you can create solutions that meet business needs and deliver measurable value. As you progress through this book, you'll gain the knowledge and tools needed to excel as an IT Solutions Architect.

Additional Resources

- Project Management Institute (PMI) (Project Management Institute | PMI)
- Coursera - Project Management Courses (coursera.org/browse/business/project-management)
- Harvard Business Review - Leadership Skills (Leadership - HBR)

- MindTools - Decision-Making Techniques (Improving Decision-Making: Techniques, Tools and Tips (mindtools.com)

Chapter 5: Soft Skills and Stakeholder Management for IT Solutions Architects

5.1. Introduction to Soft Skills for IT Solutions Architects

While technical expertise is crucial, soft skills are equally important for IT Solutions Architects. These skills enable effective communication, collaboration, and stakeholder management, ensuring that technical solutions align with business goals and deliver value. This chapter explores the key soft skills required and provides practical strategies for mastering them.

5.2. Communication Skills

Effective communication is the cornerstone of an IT Solutions Architect's role. It involves conveying complex technical concepts to non-technical stakeholders and ensuring alignment between business and technical teams.

5.2.1. Key Areas of Focus

5.2.1.1. Clarity and Simplicity:

a. Breaking down complex concepts into simple, understandable terms.

b. Example: Using analogies to explain microservices architecture to business stakeholders.

5.2.1.2. Active Listening

a. Paying attention to stakeholder concerns and feedback.

b. Example: Conducting workshops to gather input from various departments.

5.2.1.3. Visual Communication

a. Using diagrams, flowcharts, and prototypes to illustrate ideas.

b. Example: Creating an architecture diagram to explain the proposed solution to senior management.

5.2.2. Real-Life Example

A retail company's IT Solutions Architect used visual communication to present a new e-commerce platform design. By creating a detailed architecture diagram and a clickable prototype, the architect ensured that stakeholders understood the benefits and functionality of the proposed solution.

5.3. Collaboration and Teamwork

IT Solutions Architects often work with cross-functional teams, including developers, business analysts, and project managers. Collaboration skills are essential for fostering teamwork and ensuring project success.

5.3.1. Key Areas of Focus

5.3.1.1.   Building Trust

    a. Establishing credibility and reliability with team members.

    b. Example: Delivering on commitments and providing regular updates.

5.3.1.2.   Conflict Resolution

    a. Addressing disagreements and finding mutually acceptable solutions.

    b. Example: Mediating a conflict between the development and marketing teams over feature priorities.

5.3.1.3.   Facilitation

a. Leading meetings and workshops to gather input and make decisions.

b. Example: Facilitating a requirements gathering workshop with stakeholders from different departments.

5.3.2. Real-Life Example

A healthcare organisation's IT Solutions Architect facilitated a series of workshops to gather input from doctors, nurses, and administrators for a new patient management system. By fostering collaboration and addressing concerns, the architect ensured that the final solution met the needs of all stakeholders.

5.4. Stakeholder Management

Stakeholder management involves identifying, engaging, and managing the expectations of individuals and groups affected by the project. Effective stakeholder management ensures alignment and support throughout the project lifecycle.

5.4.1. Key Areas of Focus

5.4.1.1.   Stakeholder Identification
a. Identifying all individuals and groups affected by the project.
b. Example: Creating a stakeholder map to visualise key stakeholders and their interests.

5.4.1.2.   Engagement Strategies
a. Developing tailored communication and engagement plans for each stakeholder group.
b. Example: Providing regular updates to senior management and detailed technical documentation for the development team.

5.4.1.3.   Expectation Management
a. Setting realistic expectations and managing changes throughout the project.
b. Example: Using a change management process to handle scope changes and ensure stakeholder buy-in.

5.4.2. Real-Life Example
A financial institution's IT Solutions Architect managed stakeholder expectations for a new mobile banking app by providing regular

updates and involving stakeholders in key decisions. By maintaining

transparency and addressing concerns promptly, the architect

ensured stakeholder support throughout the project.

5.5. <u>Problem-Solving and Critical Thinking</u>

IT Solutions Architects must be adept at solving complex problems

and making informed decisions. Critical thinking skills enable

architects to analyse situations, evaluate options, and choose the

best course of action.

5.5.1. Key Areas of Focus

5.5.1.1.   Analytical Thinking

   a. Breaking down problems into smaller, manageable
    components.

   b. Example: Analysing the root cause of a system outage and
    proposing preventive measures.

5.5.1.2.   Decision-Making

   a. Evaluating options and making informed decisions based on
    data and analysis.

   b. Example: Choosing between cloud providers based on cost,
    scalability, and compliance requirements.

5.5.1.3.   Innovation

    a. Thinking creatively to develop innovative solutions.

    b. Example: Proposing a blockchain-based solution for secure transactions in a financial application.

5.5.2. Real-Life Example

A logistics company's IT Solutions Architect used critical thinking to address a bottleneck in its supply chain management system. By analysing the problem and evaluating various options, the architect proposed a solution that improved efficiency and reduced costs.

5.6. Leadership and Influence

IT Solutions Architects often play a leadership role, guiding teams and influencing stakeholders to achieve project goals. Leadership skills are essential for inspiring confidence and driving success.

5.6.1. Key Areas of Focus

5.6.1.1.   Vision and Strategy

    a. Articulating a clear vision and strategy for the project.

    b. Example: Presenting a roadmap for the implementation of a new IT system.

5.6.1.2. *Influence and Persuasion*

    a. Convincing stakeholders to support the proposed solution.

    b. Example: Using data and case studies to demonstrate the benefits of a cloud migration.

5.6.1.3. *Mentorship*

    a. Guiding and mentoring team members to develop their skills.

    b. Example: Providing training and support to junior developers on best practices for system design.

5.6.2. Real-Life Example

A telecommunications company's IT Solutions Architect led a team to implement a new billing system. By articulating a clear vision, influencing stakeholders, and mentoring team members, the architect ensured the project's success and delivered significant cost savings.

5.7. Interactive Features and Exercises

To help readers engage with the content and apply the concepts, this chapter includes the following interactive elements:

5.7.1.1. Scenario-Based Exercise

a. Scenario: You are an IT Solutions Architect for a retail company planning to launch a new mobile app. The app must integrate with the existing e-commerce platform and support features like personalised recommendations and secure payments.

b. Task: Outline the key steps you would take to design the solution architecture. Consider scalability, security, and user experience.

5.7.1.2. Reflection Prompt

a. Question: Think about a project you've worked on or observed. What were the key challenges during the design and implementation phases, and how could they have been addressed?

5.7.1.3. Checklist for Designing Effective Architectures

a. Understand the organisation's business goals and technical constraints.

  c. Choose the right methodology or framework for the project.

  d. Design for modularity, scalability, security, performance, and maintainability.

  e. Test the architecture with real-world scenarios and iterate as needed.

5.7.2. Real-World Case Studies

To provide deeper context, this chapter includes additional case studies from various industries:

5.7.2.1. Finance

A bank needed to modernise its legacy systems to improve customer experience and reduce costs. The IT Solutions Architect designed a cloud-based architecture that enabled real-time transactions and reduced infrastructure costs by 30%.

5.7.2.2. Education

A university wanted to create a unified platform for online learning, student management, and administrative tasks. The Solutions Architect proposed a modular architecture that integrated existing systems and provided a seamless experience for students and staff.

5.7.2.3.   Manufacturing

A car manufacturer sought to implement an IoT-based system for predictive maintenance. The Solutions Architect designed a scalable architecture that collected data from sensors and used machine learning to predict equipment failures, reducing downtime by 20%.

5.8. Conclusion

Soft skills and stakeholder management are essential for IT Solutions Architects to succeed in their roles. By mastering communication, collaboration, problem-solving, and leadership, architects can ensure that technical solutions align with business goals and deliver measurable value. As you progress through this book, you'll gain the knowledge and tools needed to excel as an IT Solutions Architect.

Additional Resources

- Project Management Institute (PMI) (Project Management Institute | PMI)
- Coursera - Project Management Courses (coursera.org/browse/business/project-management)
- Harvard Business Review - Leadership Skills (Leadership - HBR)

- MindTools - Decision-Making Techniques (Improving Decision-Making: Techniques, Tools and Tips (mindtools.com)

- Time Management Tips and Techniques (18 Time Management Tips to Boost Productivity [2024] • Asana)

Chapter 6: Business Analysis and Requirements Gathering

6.1. Introduction to Business Analysis and Requirements Gathering

Business analysis and requirements gathering are foundational activities for IT Solutions Architects. These processes ensure that technical solutions align with business goals, address stakeholder needs, and deliver measurable value. This chapter explores the role of IT Solutions Architects in business analysis, techniques for requirements elicitation, and strategies for translating business needs into technical solutions.

6.2. Role of IT Solutions Architects in Business Analysis

IT Solutions Architects play a pivotal role in bridging the gap between business stakeholders and technical teams. Their involvement in business analysis ensures that IT solutions are not only technically sound but also aligned with organisational objectives.

6.2.1. Key Aspects of Business Analysis

6.2.1.1. Understanding Business Goals

a. Collaborating with stakeholders to understand their strategic objectives, challenges, and opportunities.

b. Example: A retail company aims to increase online sales by 20% within the next year. The IT Solutions Architect works with marketing, sales, and IT teams to identify how technology can support this goal.

6.2.1.2. Identifying Requirements

a. Analysing business processes, workflows, and systems to identify gaps and opportunities for improvement.

b. Example: A healthcare provider identifies inefficiencies in its patient appointment scheduling system and seeks a solution to streamline the process.

6.2.1.3. Aligning Technical Solutions

a. Translating business requirements into technical specifications and architectural designs.

b. Example: An IT Solutions Architect designs a cloud-based e-commerce platform that supports the retail company's goal of increasing online sales.

6.2.2. Real-Life Example

An IT Solutions Architect working on a project to implement a new e-commerce platform conducts interviews and workshops with business stakeholders to understand their requirements. By actively engaging with stakeholders and conducting a thorough analysis, the architect identifies key features and functionality needed to support the organisation's online sales strategy. For instance, stakeholders highlight the need for a personalised recommendation engine and seamless integration with the existing inventory management system.

6.3. Techniques for Requirements Elicitation and Analysis

Effective requirements elicitation and analysis are critical for ensuring that IT solutions meet stakeholder needs. IT Solutions Architects can employ a variety of techniques to gather and analyse requirements.

6.3.1. Key Techniques

6.3.1.1. Interviews

    a. Conducting one-on-one or group interviews with stakeholders to gather insights into their needs, preferences, and pain points.

    b. Example: An IT Solutions Architect interviews store managers to understand their challenges with the current point-of-sale (POS) system.

6.3.1.2. Workshops

    a. Facilitating interactive workshops with cross-functional teams to brainstorm ideas, prioritise requirements, and reach consensus on project scope.

    b. Example: A logistics company organises a workshop with representatives from operations, IT, and customer service to define requirements for a new fleet management system.

6.3.1.3. Surveys and Questionnaires

    a. Distributing surveys and questionnaires to stakeholders to collect feedback and gather quantitative data on user preferences and expectations.

b. Example: A university uses a survey to gather input from students and faculty on desired features for a new online learning platform.

6.3.1.3. *Prototyping*

a. Building prototypes or mockups to visualise proposed solutions and validate requirements with stakeholders.

b. Example: An IT Solutions Architect creates a clickable prototype of a mobile app to demonstrate its functionality to business stakeholders.

6.3.2. Real-Life Example

In preparation for a system upgrade project, an IT Solutions Architect organises a requirements-gathering workshop with representatives from various departments. Through collaborative discussions and hands-on activities, the architect elicits requirements, captures feedback, and gains consensus on key features and functionality for the new system. For example, the finance team highlights the need for real-time reporting, while the operations team emphasises the importance of user-friendly interfaces.

6.4. Translating Business Needs into Technical Solutions

Once business requirements are identified and analysed, IT Solutions Architects are responsible for translating these needs into technical solutions. This involves designing architectures, selecting technologies, and ensuring alignment with business goals.

6.4.1. Key Considerations

6.4.1.1. Architecture Design:

a. Developing architectural designs and blueprints that outline the structure, components, and interactions of the proposed IT solution.

b. Example: An IT Solutions Architect designs a microservices-based architecture for an e-commerce platform, enabling independent deployment of features like product search and payment processing.

6.4.1.2. Technology Selection:

a. Evaluating and selecting appropriate technologies, platforms, and tools based on business requirements, technical constraints, and industry best practices.

   b. Example: A healthcare provider chooses a cloud-based platform for its telemedicine solution due to its scalability and compliance with data privacy regulations.

6.4.1.3.   *Risk Assessment*

   a. Assessing the risks and potential impacts associated with different architectural decisions and proposing mitigation strategies to address them.

   b. Example: An IT Solutions Architect identifies potential security risks in a proposed IoT-based solution and recommends encryption and access controls to mitigate them.

6.4.1.4.   *Alignment with Standards:*

   a. Ensuring that architectural designs adhere to industry standards, regulatory requirements, and organisational policies.

   b. Example: A financial institution ensures that its new mobile banking app complies with PCI DSS standards for payment security.

6.4.2. Real-Life Example

An IT Solutions Architect tasked with modernising an organisation's legacy HR system conducts a comprehensive review of business requirements and technical constraints. Based on this analysis, the architect proposes a cloud-based solution leveraging microservices architecture and containerisation to improve scalability, reliability, and maintainability. The new system reduces processing times for payroll and employee onboarding by 30%.

6.5. Interactive Features and Exercises

To help readers engage with the content and apply the concepts, this chapter includes the following interactive elements:

6.5.1.1. Scenario-Based Exercise

a. Scenario: You are an IT Solutions Architect for a retail company planning to implement a new inventory management system. The system must integrate with the existing e-commerce platform and support real-time stock updates.

b. Task: Outline the key steps you would take to gather requirements and design the solution architecture. Consider scalability, security, and user experience.

6.5.1.2.   *Reflection Prompt*

a. Question: Think about a project you've worked on or observed. What were the key challenges during the requirements gathering phase, and how could they have been addressed?

6.5.1.3.   *Checklist for Effective Requirements Gathering*

a. Identify and engage key stakeholders.

b. Use a combination of techniques (e.g., interviews, workshops, surveys) to gather requirements.

c. Document and prioritise requirements based on business goals.

d. Validate requirements with stakeholders through prototypes or mockups.

6.5.2. Real-World Case Studies

To provide deeper context, this chapter includes additional case studies from various industries:

6.5.2.1.   *Healthcare*

A hospital needed a new patient management system to handle increasing patient loads and comply with data privacy regulations. The IT Solutions Architect conducted stakeholder interviews and workshops to gather requirements, resulting in a cloud-based solution that improved data accessibility and reduced administrative overhead.

6.5.2.2.   Retail

A fashion retailer wanted to enhance its online shopping experience. The IT Solutions Architect used surveys and prototyping to gather feedback from customers and designed a microservices-based architecture that enabled rapid deployment of new features.

6.5.2.3.   Finance

A bank sought to modernise its legacy systems to improve customer experience and reduce costs. The IT Solutions Architect facilitated workshops with stakeholders and proposed a cloud-based architecture that enabled real-time transactions and reduced infrastructure costs by 30%.

6.6. Conclusion

Business analysis and requirements gathering are critical for ensuring that IT solutions align with business goals and deliver measurable value. By mastering these processes, IT Solutions Architects can design solutions that meet stakeholder needs and drive organisational success. As you progress through this book, you'll gain the knowledge and tools needed to excel as an IT Solutions Architect.

Additional Resources

- International Institute of Business Analysis (IIBA) (Business Analysis | The Global Standard | IIBA®)
- Business Analysis Body of Knowledge (BABOK) (Business Analysis Body of Knowledge (BABOK): Complete Guide (knowledgehut.com)
- Coursera - Business Analysis Courses (coursera.org/browse/business/business-analysis)

Chapter 7: Solution Design and Architecture Development

7.1. Introduction to Solution Design and Architecture Development

Solution design and architecture development are at the heart of an IT Solutions Architect's role. This phase involves transforming business requirements into a detailed technical blueprint that guides the development and implementation of IT systems. This chapter explores the key steps, tools, and techniques for designing effective solutions and developing robust architectures.

7.2. Key Steps in Solution Design

Solution design is a structured process that ensures the final system meets business needs and technical requirements. It involves several key steps:

7.2.1. Key Steps

7.2.1.1. Requirement Analysis

a. Reviewing and refining business requirements to ensure clarity and completeness.

b. Example: An IT Solutions Architect works with stakeholders to prioritise features for a new customer relationship management (CRM) system.

7.2.1.2. Conceptual Design

a. Creating high-level designs that outline the system's structure, components, and interactions.

b. Example: A retail company's IT Solutions Architect designs a conceptual model for an e-commerce platform, including user interfaces, databases, and integration points.

7.2.1.3. Logical Design

a. Developing detailed designs that specify how the system will function, including data flows, processes, and interfaces.

b. Example: A healthcare provider's IT Solutions Architect creates a logical design for a telemedicine platform, detailing how patient data will be stored and accessed.

7.2.1.4. Physical Design

a. Translating logical designs into technical specifications, including hardware, software, and network requirements.

b. Example: A logistics company's IT Solutions Architect specifies the servers, databases, and APIs needed for a real-time tracking system.

7.2.2. Real-Life Example

A financial institution needed a new mobile banking app to improve customer experience. The IT Solutions Architect followed a structured design process, starting with requirement analysis and ending with a physical design that included cloud-based servers, encryption protocols, and user-friendly interfaces. The final app increased mobile transactions by 25%.

7.3. Tools and Techniques for Architecture Development

IT Solutions Architects use a variety of tools and techniques to develop robust architectures. These tools help visualise, document, and communicate architectural designs.

7.3.1. Key Tools and Techniques

7.3.1.1.   Architecture Frameworks

a. Using frameworks like TOGAF, Zachman, or ArchiMate to structure and document architectural designs.

b. Example: A manufacturing company uses TOGAF to align its IT systems with business goals, resulting in a 20% increase in operational efficiency.

7.3.1.2.   Modelling Tools

a. Leveraging tools like UML, BPMN, and ERD to create visual representations of system components and processes.

b. Example: A retail company uses UML diagrams to design a microservices-based architecture for its e-commerce platform.

7.3.1.3.   Prototyping

a. Building prototypes to validate design decisions and gather feedback from stakeholders.

b. Example: A healthcare provider creates a prototype of a patient management system to demonstrate its functionality to doctors and administrators.

7.3.1.4. *Simulation and Testing*

a. Using simulation tools to test system performance and identify potential bottlenecks.

b. Example: A logistics company simulates its real-time tracking system to ensure it can handle peak loads during holiday seasons.

7.3.2. *Real-Life Example*

A telecommunications company used ArchiMate to document its network architecture, enabling better communication between technical teams and stakeholders. The visual representation helped identify inefficiencies and optimise network performance.

7.4. Best Practices for Solution Design

Following best practices ensures that solution designs are robust, scalable, and maintainable. These practices help IT Solutions Architects create systems that deliver long-term value.

7.4.1. Key Best Practices

7.4.1.1.   Modularity

a. Designing systems as independent, reusable components to improve flexibility and maintainability.

b. Example: A retail company uses a modular architecture to separate its inventory management system from its payment gateway.

7.4.1.2.   Scalability

a. Ensuring systems can handle increased loads without performance degradation.

b. Example: A streaming service uses cloud-based auto-scaling to accommodate millions of users during peak hours.

7.4.1.3.   Security

a. Incorporating security measures at every stage of the design process.

b. Example: A healthcare provider implements encryption and multi-factor authentication to secure patient data.

7.4.1.4.   Performance Optimisation

    a. Designing systems for speed and efficiency, using techniques like caching and load balancing.

    b. Example: An e-commerce platform uses content delivery networks (CDNs) to reduce page load times.

7.4.2. Real-Life Example

A financial institution adopted a microservices architecture for its online banking platform, enabling independent deployment of features like account management and fraud detection. The modular design improved scalability and reduced downtime by 30%.

7.5.   <u>Industry-Specific Applications</u>

Solution design and architecture development vary across industries, reflecting unique requirements and challenges.

7.5.1. Industry-Specific Examples

7.5.1.1.   Healthcare

A hospital needed a patient management system that could handle increasing patient loads and comply with data privacy regulations.

The IT Solutions Architect designed a cloud-based system with encryption and access controls, ensuring compliance with GDPR and HIPAA.

7.5.1.2.   Retail

A fashion retailer wanted to enhance its online shopping experience. The Solutions Architect proposed a microservices-based architecture, enabling rapid deployment of features like virtual try-ons and AI-driven product recommendations.

7.5.1.3.   Logistics

A logistics company sought to implement an IoT-based system for real-time tracking. The Solutions Architect designed a scalable architecture that collected data from sensors and used machine learning to optimise delivery routes.

7.5.2. Real-Life Example

A telecommunications company implemented a software-defined networking (SDN) solution to improve network agility and flexibility. By centralising network control, the company reduced configuration errors and improved service delivery.

7.6. <u>Interactive Features and Exercises</u>

To help readers engage with the content and apply the concepts, this chapter includes the following interactive elements:

7.6.1.1. *Scenario-Based Exercise*

a. Scenario: You are an IT Solutions Architect for a retail company planning to implement a new inventory management system. The system must integrate with the existing e-commerce platform and support real-time stock updates.

b. Task: Outline the key steps you would take to design the solution architecture. Consider scalability, security, and user experience.

7.6.1.2. *Reflection Prompt*

a. Question: Think about a system you've used or observed. How does it align with the core principles of solution design? What improvements would you suggest?

7.6.1.3. *Checklist for Effective Solution Design*

a. Understand and document business requirements.

b. Choose the right architecture framework and tools.

c. Design for modularity, scalability, security, and performance.

d. Validate the design with stakeholders and iterate as needed.

7.7. Real-World Case Studies

To provide deeper context, this chapter includes additional case studies from various industries:

7.7.1.1.   Finance

A bank needed to modernise its legacy systems to improve customer experience and reduce costs. The IT Solutions Architect designed a cloud-based architecture that enabled real-time transactions and reduced infrastructure costs by 30%.

7.7.1.2.   Education

A university wanted to create a unified platform for online learning, student management, and administrative tasks. The Solutions Architect proposed a modular architecture that integrated existing systems and provided a seamless experience for students and staff.

7.7.1.3.   Manufacturing

A car manufacturer sought to implement an IoT-based system for predictive maintenance. The Solutions Architect designed a scalable architecture that collected data from sensors and used machine learning to predict equipment failures, reducing downtime by 20%.

7.8. Conclusion

Solution design and architecture development are critical for creating IT systems that meet business needs and deliver measurable value. By following best practices, leveraging industry-specific insights, and using the right tools and techniques, IT Solutions Architects can design solutions that are robust, scalable, and future-proof. As you progress through this book, you'll gain the knowledge and tools needed to excel as an IT Solutions Architect.

Additional Resources

- AWS Well-Architected Framework (AWS Well-Architected - Build secure, efficient cloud applications (amazon.com))
- Azure Architecture Center (Azure Architecture Center - Azure Architecture Center | Microsoft Learn)
- Google Cloud Architecture Center (Cloud Architecture Guidance and Topologies | Google Cloud)

Chapter 8: Integration and Implementation

8.1. Introduction to Integration and Implementation

Integration and implementation are critical phases in the lifecycle of IT solutions. They ensure that systems work seamlessly together and are deployed efficiently to meet business needs. This chapter explores integration patterns, deployment strategies, and best practices for monitoring, testing, and quality assurance.

8.2. Integration Patterns and Best Practices

Integration is key to ensuring that diverse systems and applications work seamlessly together. IT Solutions Architects must choose the right integration patterns and follow best practices to achieve scalability, flexibility, and reliability.

8.2.1. Key Integration Patterns

8.2.1.1.   Point-to-Point Integration:

a. Direct connections between individual systems, suitable for simple integrations but prone to scalability issues.

b. Example: A small business connects its CRM system directly to its email marketing tool for customer outreach.

8.2.1.2.   Hub-and-Spoke Integration

a. Centralised integration hub (middleware) that connects multiple systems, offering greater scalability and flexibility.

b. Example: A retail company uses middleware to integrate its e-commerce platform, inventory management system, and payment gateway.

8.2.1.3.   Event-Driven Architecture

a. Decoupled communication between systems based on events, enabling asynchronous and loosely coupled integration.

b. Example: A logistics company uses event-driven architecture to trigger real-time updates in its tracking system when a package is scanned.

8.2.1.4.   API-Led Connectivity

a. Designing APIs to expose backend services and facilitate integration with external systems in a modular and reusable manner.

b. Example: A healthcare provider uses APIs to integrate its patient management system with third-party telemedicine platforms.

8.2.2. Real-Life Example

A retail company implemented an event-driven architecture for its e-commerce platform. When a customer places an order, an event is triggered, which initiates downstream processes such as inventory updates, payment processing, and order fulfilment. This approach ensured timely and efficient order management, reducing processing times by 25%.

8.3. Deployment Strategies and Release Management

Efficient deployment strategies and release management practices are essential for deploying changes to production environments with minimal disruption. IT Solutions Architects must choose the right strategy based on the system's complexity and business requirements.

8.3.1. Key Deployment Strategies

8.3.1.1. Continuous Integration (CI) and Continuous Deployment (CD):

a. Automating the build, test, and deployment process to deliver changes rapidly and reliably.

b. Example: A software development team uses Jenkins and GitLab CI/CD to automate the deployment of a mobile banking app.

8.3.1.2. Blue-Green Deployment

a. Rolling out updates by gradually shifting traffic from the existing (blue) environment to the new (green) environment, minimising downtime and risk.

b. Example: A retail company uses blue-green deployment to update its e-commerce platform during peak shopping seasons.

8.3.1.3.   Canary Release

a. Deploying changes to a small subset of users or servers first to validate functionality and gather feedback before full rollout.

b. Example: A healthcare provider tests a new telemedicine feature with a select group of doctors before making it available to all users.

8.3.1.4.   Rollback and Rollforward Strategies

a. Having mechanisms in place to revert to a previous state (rollback) or apply fixes and move forward (rollforward) in case of deployment failures.

b. Example: A financial institution implements rollback mechanisms for its online banking platform to ensure minimal disruption during updates.

8.3.2. Real-Life Example

A software development team adopted a CI/CD pipeline using tools like Jenkins and GitLab CI/CD to automate the build and deployment process. Changes were continuously integrated, tested, and deployed to production, ensuring rapid and reliable delivery of new features and updates. This approach reduced deployment times from weeks to hours.

8.4. Monitoring, Testing, and Quality Assurance

Monitoring, testing, and quality assurance are critical for ensuring the reliability, performance, and security of IT solutions. IT Solutions Architects must implement robust practices to maintain high standards.

8.4.1. Key Practices

8.4.1.1. Performance Monitoring

a. Tracking system metrics and key performance indicators (KPIs) to identify bottlenecks and optimise performance.

b. Example: A retail company uses AWS CloudWatch to monitor its e-commerce platform and optimise server performance.

8.4.1.2. Automated Testing

a. Implementing automated testing frameworks and scripts to validate functionality, detect regressions, and ensure code quality.

b. Example: A logistics company uses Selenium for automated testing of its real-time tracking system.

8.4.1.3.   Security Testing

a. Conducting regular security assessments, vulnerability scans, and penetration testing to identify and remediate security vulnerabilities.

b. Example: A healthcare provider conducts quarterly penetration tests to ensure its telemedicine platform complies with data privacy regulations.

8.4.1.4.   Quality Assurance (QA) Processes

a. Establishing QA processes and standards to ensure that deliverables meet quality requirements and user expectations.

b. Example: A financial institution implements a QA process that includes code reviews, automated testing, and user acceptance testing (UAT).

8.4.2. Real-Life Example

A financial institution implemented comprehensive monitoring and testing practices for its online banking platform. Performance metrics such as response time and error rates were monitored continuously. At the same time, automated regression tests and security scans were conducted as part of the CI/CD pipeline to maintain high levels of reliability and security. This approach reduced system outages by 30% and improved customer satisfaction.

8.5. Interactive Features and Exercises

To help readers engage with the content and apply the concepts, this chapter includes the following interactive elements:

8.5.1.1. Scenario-Based Exercise

a. Scenario: You are an IT Solutions Architect for a retail company planning to implement a new inventory management system. The system must integrate with the existing e-commerce platform and support real-time stock updates.

b. Task: Outline the key steps you would take to design the integration and deployment strategy. Consider scalability, security, and user experience.

8.5.1.2. Reflection Prompt

a. Question: Think about a system you've used or observed. How does it align with the core principles of integration and deployment? What improvements would you suggest?

8.5.1.3.   Checklist for Successful Integration and Implementation:

a. Choose the right integration pattern based on system requirements.

b. Select an appropriate deployment strategy to minimise risks and disruptions.

c. Implement robust monitoring, testing, and quality assurance practices.

d. Gather feedback and continuously improve the system post-deployment.

8.6.   Real-World Case Studies

To provide deeper context, this chapter includes additional case studies from various industries:

8.6.1.1.   Finance

A bank needed to modernise its legacy systems to improve customer experience and reduce costs. The IT Solutions Architect designed a cloud-based architecture that enabled real-time transactions and reduced infrastructure costs by 30%.

8.6.1.2.   Education

A university wanted to create a unified platform for online learning, student management, and administrative tasks. The Solutions

Architect proposed a modular architecture that integrated existing systems and provided a seamless experience for students and staff.

8.6.1.3. *Manufacturing*

A car manufacturer sought to implement an IoT-based system for predictive maintenance. The Solutions Architect designed a scalable architecture that collected data from sensors and used machine learning to predict equipment failures, reducing downtime by 20%.

8.7. <u>Conclusion</u>

Integration and implementation are critical for ensuring that IT solutions meet business needs and deliver measurable value. By following best practices, leveraging the right tools, and engaging stakeholders, IT Solutions Architects can ensure successful delivery of systems that are reliable, scalable, and secure. As you progress through this book, you'll gain the knowledge and tools needed to excel as an IT Solutions Architect.

Additional Resources

- AWS Integration Patterns (Enterprise Integration Patterns | AWS Compute Blog (amazon.com))
- Azure Integration Patterns (Integration architecture design - Azure Architecture Center | Microsoft Learn)

- Google Cloud Integration Patterns (Application Integration overview | Google Cloud)

Chapter 9: Emerging Technologies and Trends in IT Solutions Architecture

9.1. Introduction to Emerging Technologies and Trends

The field of IT Solutions Architecture is constantly evolving, driven by advancements in technology and changing business needs. This chapter explores the latest trends and emerging technologies that are shaping the future of solution architecture. By staying informed about these developments, IT Solutions Architects can design innovative solutions that deliver value and keep their organisations competitive.

9.2. Artificial Intelligence and Machine Learning

Artificial Intelligence (AI) and Machine Learning (ML) are transforming the way organisations operate, enabling automation, predictive analytics, and intelligent decision-making.

9.2.1. Key Areas of Focus

9.2.1.1. AI-Driven Automation

a. Using AI to automate repetitive tasks and improve efficiency.

b. Example: A retail company uses AI-powered chatbots to handle customer inquiries, reducing response times and improving customer satisfaction.

9.2.1.2. Predictive Analytics

a. Leveraging ML algorithms to analyse data and make predictions.

b. Example: A healthcare provider uses predictive analytics to identify patients at risk of chronic diseases and provide early interventions.

9.2.1.3. Intelligent Decision-Making

a. Using AI to support decision-making processes with data-driven insights.

b. Example: A financial institution uses AI to assess credit risk and make lending decisions.

9.2.2. *Real-Life Example*

A logistics company implemented an AI-powered route optimisation system that reduced delivery times by 15% and fuel costs by 10%. The system analysed historical data and real-time traffic information to determine the most efficient routes.

9.3. Internet of Things (IoT)

The Internet of Things (IoT) is connecting devices and enabling new levels of automation and data collection. IT Solutions Architects must understand how to design systems that leverage IoT technologies.

9.3.1. *Key Areas of Focus*

9.3.1.1.   *IoT Architecture*

a. Designing systems that support the integration and management of IoT devices.

b. Example: A manufacturing company uses IoT sensors to monitor equipment performance and predict maintenance needs.

9.3.1.2.   Data Management

a. Handling the large volumes of data generated by IoT devices.

b. Example: A smart city project uses a data lake to store and analyse data from various IoT sensors, such as traffic cameras and environmental monitors.

9.3.1.3.   Security and Privacy

a. Ensuring the security and privacy of IoT devices and data.

b. Example: A healthcare provider implements encryption and access controls to protect data from wearable devices.

9.3.2. Real-Life Example

A utility company deployed an IoT-based smart grid system that improved energy distribution and reduced outages. The system used sensors to monitor grid performance and automatically reroute power during disruptions.

9.4. Edge Computing

Edge computing brings computation and data storage closer to the devices that generate and use data, reducing latency and bandwidth usage.

9.4.1. Key Areas of Focus

9.4.1.1.   Edge Architecture
a. Designing systems that distribute processing between edge devices and centralised cloud servers.
b. Example: A retail company uses edge computing to process data from in-store cameras in real-time, enabling personalised customer experiences.

9.4.1.2.   Latency Reduction
a. Reducing latency for time-sensitive applications.
b. Example: A gaming company uses edge servers to reduce latency for online multiplayer games.

9.4.1.3.   Bandwidth Optimisation
a. Reducing bandwidth usage by processing data locally.
b. Example: A manufacturing company uses edge computing to analyse sensor data on-site, reducing the need to transmit large volumes of data to the cloud.

9.4.2. Real-Life Example

A telecommunications company implemented an edge computing solution for its 5G network, reducing latency and improving the performance of real-time applications such as video streaming and online gaming.

9.5. Blockchain Technology

Blockchain technology offers secure, transparent, and decentralised solutions for various applications, from finance to supply chain management.

9.5.1. Key Areas of Focus

9.5.1.1. Decentralised Systems

   a. Designing systems that leverage blockchain for decentralised control and transparency.
   b. Example: A financial institution uses blockchain to enable secure, peer-to-peer transactions without intermediaries.

9.5.1.2. Smart Contracts

a. Using smart contracts to automate and enforce agreements.

b.   Example: A real estate company uses smart contracts to automate property transactions, reducing paperwork and processing times.

9.5.1.3. *Supply Chain Transparency*

a. Using blockchain to track and verify the provenance of goods.

b. Example: A retail company uses blockchain to ensure the authenticity of luxury goods and prevent counterfeiting.

9.5.2. Real-Life Example

A food company implemented a blockchain-based supply chain tracking system that improved transparency and traceability. Consumers could scan a QR code on product packaging to view the entire supply chain history, from farm to store.

9.6. Quantum Computing

Quantum computing promises to revolutionise computing by solving complex problems that are currently intractable for classical computers.

9.6.1. Key Areas of Focus

9.6.1.1. Quantum Algorithms

a. Understanding quantum algorithms and their potential applications.

b. Example: A pharmaceutical company uses quantum computing to accelerate drug discovery by simulating molecular interactions.

9.6.1.2. Quantum Security

a. Exploring the impact of quantum computing on cryptography and security.

b. Example: A financial institution evaluates post-quantum cryptographic algorithms to protect sensitive data from future quantum attacks.

9.6.1.3. Hybrid Systems

a. Designing systems that integrate classical and quantum computing.

b. Example: A logistics company uses a hybrid system to optimise complex routing problems, combining classical optimisation techniques with quantum algorithms.

9.6.2. Real-Life Example

A research institution partnered with a quantum computing company to develop a hybrid system for optimising energy distribution in a smart grid. The system used quantum algorithms to solve complex optimisation problems and classical algorithms for real-time control.

9.7. Interactive Features and Exercises

To help readers engage with the content and apply the concepts, this chapter includes the following interactive elements:

9.7.1.1. Scenario-Based Exercise

a. Scenario: You are an IT Solutions Architect for a retail company planning to implement an AI-powered recommendation system. The system must analyse customer behaviour and provide personalised product recommendations in real-time.

b. Task: Outline the key steps you would take to design the solution architecture. Consider scalability, security, and user experience.

9.7.1.2. Reflection Prompt

a. Question: Think about a project you've worked on or observed. How could emerging technologies like AI, IoT, or blockchain have improved the solution?

9.7.1.3. Checklist for Adopting Emerging Technologies

a. Understand the organisation's business goals and technical constraints.

b. Evaluate the potential benefits and risks of adopting emerging technologies.

c. Develop a roadmap for integrating emerging technologies into existing systems.

b. Monitor industry trends and stay informed about new developments.

9.8. Real-World Case Studies

To provide deeper context, this chapter includes additional case studies from various industries:

9.8.1.1. Healthcare

A hospital implemented an AI-powered diagnostic system that improved the accuracy of disease detection and reduced diagnostic errors by 20%.

9.8.1.2.   Retail

A fashion retailer used IoT sensors to track inventory in real-time, reducing stockouts and improving supply chain efficiency.

9.8.1.3.   Finance

A bank adopted blockchain technology to streamline cross-border payments, reducing transaction times from days to minutes.

9.9. Conclusion

Emerging technologies and trends are reshaping the field of IT Solutions Architecture, offering new opportunities for innovation and value creation. By staying informed about these developments and understanding how to leverage them, IT Solutions Architects can design solutions that meet the evolving needs of their organisations. As you progress through this book, you'll gain the knowledge and tools needed to excel as an IT Solutions Architect.

Additional Resources

- Microsoft Learn: Emerging Technologies (Microsoft Research – Emerging Technology, Computer, and Software Research)

- AWS Emerging Tech (What's New at AWS – Cloud Innovation & News (amazon.com))
- Google Cloud AI & Machine Learning (Machine Learning & AI Courses | Google Cloud Training)

Chapter 10: Maintenance, Optimisation, and Continuous Improvement of IT Solutions

10.1. Introduction to Maintenance, Optimisation, and Continuous Improvement

Once an IT solution is deployed, the work doesn't stop. Maintenance, optimisation, and continuous improvement are essential for ensuring that systems remain reliable, efficient, and aligned with evolving business needs. This chapter explores the key practices and strategies for maintaining and enhancing IT solutions over their lifecycle.

10.2. Maintenance Strategies for IT Solutions

Maintenance ensures that systems continue to function as intended and remain secure and up-to-date. IT Solutions Architects must implement proactive and reactive maintenance strategies to address issues and prevent downtime.

10.2.1.   Key Maintenance Strategies

10.2.1.1.   Preventive Maintenance

a. Regularly updating software, applying patches, and performing system checks to prevent issues.

b. Example: A retail company schedules monthly updates for its e-commerce platform to address security vulnerabilities.

10.2.1.2.   Corrective Maintenance

a. Fixing issues as they arise to restore system functionality.

b. Example: A healthcare provider resolves a bug in its telemedicine platform that caused video calls to drop.

10.2.1.3.   Adaptive Maintenance

a. Modifying systems to accommodate changes in business requirements or technology.

b. Example: A logistics company updates its real-time tracking system to support new IoT devices.

10.2.1.4.   Perfective Maintenance

a. Enhancing system performance, usability, and functionality based on user feedback.

b. Example: A financial institution improves the user interface of its mobile banking app to enhance customer experience.

10.2.2.   *Real-Life Example*

A telecommunications company implemented a preventive maintenance strategy for its billing system, including regular updates and performance checks. This approach reduced system outages by 25% and improved customer satisfaction.

10.3. Optimisation Techniques for IT Solutions

Optimisation ensures that systems operate efficiently and deliver maximum value. IT Solutions Architects must identify and address performance bottlenecks, resource constraints, and inefficiencies.

10.3.1.   *Key Optimisation Techniques*

10.3.1.1. *Performance Tuning*

a. Adjusting system configurations and parameters to improve performance.
b. Example: A retail company optimises its database queries to reduce page load times on its e-commerce platform.

10.3.1.2. Resource Allocation

a. Allocating resources (e.g., CPU, memory, storage) to meet system demands.

b. Example: A healthcare provider allocates additional server resources to its telemedicine platform during peak hours.

10.3.1.3. Scalability Improvements

a. Enhancing system scalability to handle increased loads.

b. Example: A logistics company implements auto-scaling for its real-time tracking system to accommodate peak delivery periods.

10.3.1.4. Cost Optimisation

a. Reducing operational costs without compromising performance or functionality.

b. Example: A financial institution migrates its data storage to a more cost-effective cloud provider.

10.3.2. Real-Life Example

A retail company optimised its e-commerce platform by implementing caching and content delivery networks (CDNs). These improvements reduced page load times by 40% and increased customer satisfaction.

10.4. Continuous Improvement Practices

Continuous improvement ensures that IT solutions evolve to meet changing business needs and technological advancements. IT Solutions Architects must foster a culture of innovation and learning.

10.4.1. Key Continuous Improvement Practices

10.4.1.1. Feedback Loops

a. Gathering feedback from users and stakeholders to identify areas for improvement.

b. Example: A healthcare provider conducts quarterly surveys with patients and doctors to gather feedback on its telemedicine platform.

10.4.1.2. Iterative Development

a. Implementing changes in small, incremental steps to minimise risk and maximise learning.

b. Example: A logistics company uses Agile methodology to continuously improve its real-time tracking system.

10.4.1.3. *Benchmarking*

a. Comparing system performance and practices against industry standards and competitors.

b. Example: A financial institution benchmarks its mobile banking app against leading competitors to identify areas for improvement.

10.4.1.4. *Innovation Initiatives*

a. Encouraging experimentation and innovation to explore new technologies and approaches.

b. Example: A retail company establishes an innovation lab to test new technologies like AI and AR for enhancing the shopping experience.

10.4.2. *Real-Life Example*

A financial institution implemented a continuous improvement program for its online banking platform. By gathering user feedback, conducting regular performance reviews, and experimenting with new features, the institution improved customer satisfaction and reduced churn by 15%.

10.5. Interactive Features and Exercises

To help readers engage with the content and apply the concepts, this chapter includes the following interactive elements:

10.5.1.1. Scenario-Based Exercise

a. Scenario: You are an IT Solutions Architect for a retail company planning to optimise its e-commerce platform. The platform must handle increased traffic during holiday seasons and provide a seamless user experience.

b. Task: Outline the key steps you would take to optimise the platform. Consider performance, scalability, and cost-efficiency.

10.5.1.2. Reflection Prompt

a. Question: Think about a system you've used or observed. What maintenance, optimisation, or continuous improvement practices were implemented? What improvements would you suggest?

10.5.1.3. Checklist for Maintenance, Optimisation, and Continuous Improvement

a. Implement preventive, corrective, adaptive, and perfective maintenance strategies.

b. Optimise system performance, resource allocation, scalability, and costs.

c. Foster a culture of continuous improvement through feedback loops, iterative development, benchmarking, and innovation initiatives.

10.6. <u>Real-World Case Studies</u>

To provide deeper context, this chapter includes additional case studies from various industries:

10.6.1.1. *Finance*

A bank needed to modernise its legacy systems to improve customer experience and reduce costs. The IT Solutions Architect designed a cloud-based architecture that enabled real-time transactions and reduced infrastructure costs by 30%.

10.6.1.2. *Education*

A university wanted to create a unified platform for online learning, student management, and administrative tasks. The Solutions Architect proposed a modular architecture that integrated existing systems and provided a seamless experience for students and staff.

10.6.1.3. Manufacturing

A car manufacturer sought to implement an IoT-based system for predictive maintenance. The Solutions Architect designed a scalable architecture that collected data from sensors and used machine learning to predict equipment failures, reducing downtime by 20%.

10.7. Conclusion

Maintenance, optimisation, and continuous improvement are essential for ensuring that IT solutions remain reliable, efficient, and aligned with business needs. By following best practices, leveraging the right tools, and fostering a culture of innovation, IT Solutions Architects can deliver systems that provide long-term value. As you progress through this book, you'll gain the knowledge and tools needed to excel as an IT Solutions Architect.

Chapter 11: Implementation, Testing, and Deployment of IT Solutions

11.1. Introduction to Implementation, Testing, and Deployment

The implementation, testing, and deployment phase is where the IT solution transitions from design to reality. This phase ensures that the system is built according to specifications, functions as intended, and is delivered to users seamlessly. This chapter explores the key steps, tools, and best practices for successfully implementing, testing, and deploying IT solutions.

11.2. Key Steps in Implementation

Implementation involves translating the architectural design into a functional system. This phase requires careful planning, coordination, and execution to ensure the solution meets business and technical requirements.

11.2.1. *Key Steps*

11.2.1.1. *Development*
a. Guiding development teams to build the system according to the design.
b. Example: A retail company uses Agile methodology to develop its e-commerce platform, with regular sprints and reviews.

11.2.1.2. *Integration*
a. Ensuring that all system components work together seamlessly.
b. Example: A logistics company integrates its real-time tracking system with third-party delivery services using APIs.

11.2.1.3. *Configuration*
a. Setting up hardware, software, and network configurations as per the design.
b. Example: A healthcare provider configures its telemedicine platform to comply with data privacy regulations.

11.2.1.4. *Documentation*
a. Creating technical documentation to guide development, testing, and maintenance.

b. Example: A financial institution documents its mobile banking app's architecture, APIs, and security protocols.

11.2.2. Real-Life Example

A telecommunications company implemented a new billing system by following a structured implementation process. The IT Solutions Architect guided the development team, ensured seamless integration with existing systems, and documented the entire process. The new system reduced billing errors by 20% and improved customer satisfaction.

11.3. Testing Strategies and Techniques

Testing is critical for ensuring that the system functions as intended and meets quality standards. IT Solutions Architects must design and oversee comprehensive testing strategies.

11.3.1. Key Testing Techniques

11.3.1.1. Unit Testing

a. Testing individual components or modules to ensure they work correctly.

b. Example: A retail company tests the payment processing module of its e-commerce platform to ensure accurate transactions.

11.3.1.2. Integration Testing

a. Testing the interactions between different system components.

b. Example: A logistics company tests the integration between its tracking system and third-party APIs.

11.3.1.3. User Acceptance Testing (UAT)

a. Testing the system with end-users to ensure it meets their needs.

b. Example: A healthcare provider conducts UAT for its patient management system with doctors and nurses.

11.3.1.4. Performance Testing

a. Testing the system's performance under various conditions, such as peak loads.

b. Example: A streaming service tests its platform to ensure it can handle millions of users during live events.

11.3.2.   *Real-Life Example*

A financial institution conducted rigorous testing for its new mobile banking app, including unit, integration, and performance testing. By involving end-users in UAT, the institution identified and resolved issues before launch, resulting in a smooth rollout and positive user feedback.

11.4. Deployment Strategies

Deployment involves delivering the system to users in a controlled and efficient manner. IT Solutions Architects must choose the right deployment strategy to minimise risks and disruptions.

11.4.1.   *Key Deployment Strategies*

11.4.1.1.   *Blue-Green Deployment*

a. Maintaining two identical environments (blue and green) and switching between them during deployment.
b. Example: A retail company uses blue-green deployment to minimise downtime during the rollout of its e-commerce platform.

11.4.1.2.   *Canary Release*

a.   Gradually rolling out the system to a small group of users before full deployment.

b.   Example: A healthcare provider uses a canary release to test its telemedicine platform with a select group of doctors before making it available to all users.

11.4.1.3.   *Rolling Deployment*

a.   Deploying the system incrementally across different servers or regions.

b.   Example: A logistics company uses rolling deployment to update its real-time tracking system across multiple regions.

11.4.1.4.   *Automated Deployment*

a.   Using automation tools to streamline the deployment process.

b.   Example: A financial institution uses CI/CD pipelines to automate the deployment of its mobile banking app.

11.4.2.   *Real-Life Example*

A telecommunications company used a blue-green deployment strategy to launch its new billing system. By maintaining two environments, the company minimised downtime and ensured a smooth transition for users.

11.5. Post-Deployment Activities

After deployment, IT Solutions Architects must monitor the system's performance, gather feedback, and make optimisations as needed.

11.5.1.　　Key Post-Deployment Activities

11.5.1.1.　Performance Monitoring

a. Using monitoring tools to track system performance and identify bottlenecks.
b. Example: A retail company uses AWS CloudWatch to monitor its e-commerce platform and optimise server performance.

11.5.1.2.　User Feedback

a. Gathering feedback from users to identify areas for improvement.
b. Example: A healthcare provider conducts surveys with patients and doctors to improve its telemedicine platform.

11.5.1.3. *Continuous Improvement*

a. Implementing changes based on feedback and performance data.

b. Example: A logistics company uses A/B testing to optimise its real-time tracking system's user interface.

11.5.2.   *Real-Life Example*

A financial institution conducted a post-implementation review of its mobile banking app and identified opportunities to improve performance. By optimising database queries and adding caching, the institution reduced response times by 40%.

11.6. Interactive Features and Exercises

To help readers engage with the content and apply the concepts, this chapter includes the following interactive elements:

11.6.1.1. *Scenario-Based Exercise*

a. Scenario: You are an IT Solutions Architect for a retail company planning to launch a new mobile app. The app must integrate with the existing e-commerce platform and support features like personalised recommendations and secure payments.

b. Task: Outline the key steps you would take to implement, test, and deploy the solution. Consider scalability, security, and user experience.

11.6.1.2. Reflection Prompt

a. Question: Think about a project you've worked on or observed. What were the key challenges during the implementation, testing, and deployment phases, and how could they have been addressed?

11.6.1.3. Checklist for Successful Implementation, Testing, and Deployment

a. Guide development teams to build the system according to the design.

b. Design and oversee comprehensive testing strategies.

c. Choose the right deployment strategy to minimise risks and disruptions.

d. Monitor system performance and gather feedback for continuous improvement.

11.7. Real-World Case Studies

To provide deeper context, this chapter includes additional case studies from various industries:

11.7.1.1. Finance

A bank needed to modernise its legacy systems to improve customer experience and reduce costs. The IT Solutions Architect designed a cloud-based architecture that enabled real-time transactions and reduced infrastructure costs by 30%.

11.7.1.2. Education

A university wanted to create a unified platform for online learning, student management, and administrative tasks. The Solutions Architect proposed a modular architecture that integrated existing systems and provided a seamless experience for students and staff.

11.7.1.3. Manufacturing

A car manufacturer sought to implement an IoT-based system for predictive maintenance. The Solutions Architect designed a scalable architecture that collected data from sensors and used machine learning to predict equipment failures, reducing downtime by 20%.

11.8. Conclusion

Implementation, testing, and deployment are critical phases in the lifecycle of an IT solution. By following best practices, leveraging the right tools, and engaging stakeholders, IT Solutions Architects can ensure successful delivery of systems that meet business needs and deliver measurable value. As you progress through this book, you'll gain the knowledge and tools needed to excel as an IT Solutions Architect.

Chapter 12: Ethics, Security, and Compliance in IT Solutions Architecture

12.1. Introduction to Ethics, Security, and Compliance

Ethics, security, and compliance are foundational pillars of IT Solutions Architecture. They ensure that systems are not only technically sound but also aligned with legal, regulatory, and ethical standards. This chapter explores the principles, challenges, and best practices for integrating ethics, security, and compliance into IT architecture.

12.2. Ethical Considerations in IT Solutions Architecture

Ethics play a critical role in ensuring that IT solutions are designed and implemented responsibly, with consideration for their impact on individuals, organisations, and society.

12.2.1.   Key Ethical Principles

12.2.1.1. Transparency

a. Ensuring that system operations and decision-making processes are transparent and understandable to users.

b. Example: A healthcare provider designs a telemedicine platform that clearly explains how patient data is used and stored.

12.2.1.2. Fairness

a. Avoiding bias and ensuring equitable treatment of all users.

b. Example: A financial institution uses AI algorithms that are regularly audited for bias to ensure fair lending practices.

12.2.1.3. Privacy

a. Protecting user data and ensuring compliance with data privacy regulations.

b. Example: A retail company implements encryption and access controls to safeguard customer information.

12.2.1.4. Accountability

a. Establishing mechanisms to hold individuals and organisations accountable for their actions.

b. Example: A logistics company implements audit trails to track changes to its real-time tracking system.

12.2.2. *Real-Life Example*

A social media platform faced criticism for using algorithms that promoted biased content. In response, the company implemented ethical guidelines for algorithm design, including regular audits and transparency reports, to ensure fairness and accountability.

12.3. Security Best Practices in IT Solutions Architecture

Security is a top priority in IT architecture, as systems must protect sensitive data and ensure operational continuity. IT Solutions Architects must implement robust security measures to mitigate risks.

12.3.1. *Key Security Practices*

12.3.1.1. *Data Encryption*

a. Encrypting data at rest and in transit to protect it from unauthorised access.

b. Example: A healthcare provider uses AES-256 encryption to secure patient data in its telemedicine platform.

12.3.1.2. Access Controls

a. Implementing role-based access controls (RBAC) to restrict access to sensitive information.

b. Example: A financial institution uses multi-factor authentication (MFA) to secure access to its online banking platform.

12.3.1.3. Threat Detection and Response

a. Deploying tools and processes to detect and respond to security threats in real-time.

b. Example: A retail company uses a SIEM (Security Information and Event Management) system to monitor its e-commerce platform for suspicious activity.

12.3.1.4. Regular Security Audits

a. Conducting regular security assessments to identify and address vulnerabilities.

b. Example: A logistics company performs quarterly penetration tests to ensure the security of its real-time tracking system.

12.3.2.   *Real-Life Example*

A financial institution implemented a comprehensive security strategy that included encryption, access controls, and regular security audits. This approach reduced security incidents by 40% and improved customer trust.

12.4. Compliance with Regulatory Standards

Compliance with regulatory standards is essential for maintaining trust, security, and legal adherence. IT Solutions Architects must ensure that systems meet all relevant requirements.

12.4.1.   *Key Regulatory Considerations*

12.4.1.1.   *Data Privacy Regulations*

a. Ensuring compliance with regulations such as GDPR, HIPAA, and CCPA.

b. Example: A healthcare provider implements data anonymisation and access controls to comply with HIPAA.

12.4.1.2. Industry Standards

a. Adhering to industry standards such as PCI DSS for payment security and ISO 27001 for information security.

b. Example: A retail company complies with PCI DSS by encrypting payment data and implementing secure payment gateways.

12.4.1.3. Auditing and Reporting

a. Conducting regular audits and assessments to demonstrate compliance and address any non-conformities.

b. Example: A financial institution conducts annual audits to ensure compliance with GDPR and PCI DSS.

12.4.1.4. Staying Updated

a. Keeping abreast of regulatory changes and updates to ensure ongoing compliance.

b. Example: A logistics company monitors updates to data protection regulations and adjusts its IT systems accordingly.

12.4.2.   Real-Life Example

A healthcare organisation implemented a compliance program that included regular audits, staff training, and updates to its IT systems.

This approach ensured compliance with HIPAA and GDPR, avoiding costly penalties and maintaining patient trust.

12.5. Interactive Features and Exercises

To help readers engage with the content and apply the concepts, this chapter includes the following interactive elements:

12.5.1.1. Scenario-Based Exercise:

a. Scenario: You are an IT Solutions Architect for a retail company planning to implement a new inventory management system. The system must comply with PCI DSS standards and integrate with the existing e-commerce platform.

b. Task: Outline the key steps you would take to ensure compliance and mitigate risks. Consider ethics, security, and regulatory requirements.

12.5.1.2. Reflection Prompt

a. Question: Think about a system you've used or observed. What ethical, security, and compliance practices were implemented? What improvements would you suggest?

12.5.1.3.   Checklist for Ethics, Security, and Compliance

a. Ensure transparency, fairness, privacy, and accountability in system design.

b. Implement robust security measures, including encryption, access controls, and threat detection.

c. Ensure compliance with regulatory standards through regular audits and updates.

12.6. Real-World Case Studies

To provide deeper context, this chapter includes additional case studies from various industries:

12.6.1.1.   Finance

A bank implemented a comprehensive security and compliance program that included encryption, access controls, and regular audits. This approach reduced security incidents by 40% and ensured compliance with GDPR and PCI DSS.

12.6.1.2.   Healthcare

A hospital adopted a telemedicine platform that complied with HIPAA and GDPR. The platform included encryption, access controls, and regular security audits, ensuring patient data privacy and security.

12.6.1.3.   *Retail*

A retail company implemented a compliance program for its e-commerce platform, including PCI DSS compliance and regular security audits. This approach improved customer trust and reduced the risk of data breaches.

12.7. Conclusion

Ethics, security, and compliance are essential for ensuring that IT solutions are not only technically sound but also aligned with legal, regulatory, and ethical standards. By following best practices, leveraging the right tools, and fostering a culture of responsibility, IT Solutions Architects can deliver systems that provide long-term value. As you progress through this book, you'll gain the knowledge and tools needed to excel as an IT Solutions Architect.

Chapter 13: The Role of IT Solutions Architects in Digital Transformation

13.1. Introduction to Digital Transformation

Digital transformation is the integration of digital technologies into all areas of an organisation, fundamentally changing how it operates and delivers value to customers. IT Solutions Architects play a pivotal role in driving and enabling this transformation by designing systems that align with business goals and leverage emerging technologies.

13.2. Key Drivers of Digital Transformation

Digital transformation is driven by several factors, including technological advancements, changing customer expectations, and competitive pressures. IT Solutions Architects must understand these drivers to design solutions that enable organisations to thrive in the digital age.

13.2.1. Key Drivers

13.2.1.1. Technological Advancements

a. The rapid evolution of technologies such as cloud computing, AI, IoT, and blockchain.

b. Example: A retail company adopts AI-powered chatbots to enhance customer service and reduce response times.

13.2.1.2. Changing Customer Expectations

a. Customers demand seamless, personalised, and efficient experiences across all touchpoints.

b. Example: A healthcare provider implements a telemedicine platform to offer convenient and accessible care to patients.

13.2.1.3. Competitive Pressures

a. Organisations must innovate and adapt to stay ahead of competitors.

b. Example: A logistics company adopts IoT and real-time tracking to improve delivery efficiency and customer satisfaction.

13.2.1.4. Operational Efficiency

a. Digital transformation enables organisations to streamline processes, reduce costs, and improve productivity.

b. Example: A financial institution automates its loan approval process using AI and machine learning.

13.2.2. *Real-Life Example*

A retail company embarked on a digital transformation journey to modernise its e-commerce platform. By adopting cloud computing, AI-driven personalisation, and IoT for inventory management, the company improved customer experience, reduced operational costs, and increased sales by 20%.

13.3. The Role of IT Solutions Architects in Digital Transformation

IT Solutions Architects are at the forefront of digital transformation, bridging the gap between business goals and technical solutions. Their role encompasses several key responsibilities:

13.3.1. *Key Responsibilities*

13.3.1.1. *Strategic Alignment*

a. Aligning IT initiatives with business goals to drive value and innovation.

b. Example: An IT Solutions Architect designs a cloud-based architecture that supports the company's goal of expanding into new markets.

13.3.1.2. Technology Selection

a. Evaluating and selecting the right technologies to enable digital transformation.

b. Example: A healthcare provider chooses a microservices architecture for its telemedicine platform to ensure scalability and flexibility.

13.3.1.3. System Integration

a. Integrating new technologies with existing systems to create a cohesive and efficient ecosystem.

b. Example: A logistics company integrates IoT sensors with its real-time tracking system to improve delivery accuracy.

13.3.1.4. Change Management

a. Facilitating organisational change by engaging stakeholders, training users, and managing resistance.

b. Example: A financial institution implements a change management program to support the adoption of a new mobile banking app.

13.3.2.   Real-Life Example

A telecommunications company hired an IT Solutions Architect to lead its digital transformation initiative. The architect designed a cloud-based architecture, integrated AI-driven analytics, and implemented a change management program. This approach improved operational efficiency, reduced costs, and enhanced customer satisfaction.

13.4. Challenges in Digital Transformation

Digital transformation is not without its challenges. IT Solutions Architects must navigate these challenges to ensure successful outcomes.

13.4.1.   Key Challenges

13.4.1.1.   Legacy Systems

a. Integrating new technologies with outdated legacy systems can be complex and costly.
b. Example: A financial institution faces challenges in migrating its legacy core banking system to the cloud.

13.4.1.2. *Organisational Resistance*

a. Employees and stakeholders may resist change due to fear of job loss or lack of understanding.

b. Example: A retail company struggles to gain buy-in from store managers for its new inventory management system.

13.4.1.3. *Security and Compliance*

a. Ensuring that digital transformation initiatives comply with regulatory standards and protect sensitive data.

b. Example: A healthcare provider must ensure that its telemedicine platform complies with HIPAA and GDPR.

13.4.1.4. *Skill Gaps*

a. Organisations may lack the skills and expertise needed to implement and manage new technologies.

b. Example: A logistics company invests in training programs to upskill its workforce in IoT and data analytics.

13.4.2. *Real-Life Example*

A manufacturing company faced challenges in adopting IoT for predictive maintenance due to legacy systems and skill gaps. The IT Solutions Architect addressed these challenges by designing a phased implementation plan, providing training programs, and ensuring compliance with industry standards.

13.5. <u>Best Practices for Successful Digital Transformation</u>

To ensure successful digital transformation, IT Solutions Architects must follow best practices that address technical, organisational, and cultural aspects.

13.5.1.   *Key Best Practices*

13.5.1.1.   *Start with a Clear Vision:*

a. Define a clear vision and strategy for digital transformation, aligned with business goals.

b. Example: A retail company defines its vision as "delivering seamless, personalised shopping experiences across all channels."

13.5.1.2.   *Engage Stakeholders*

a. Involve stakeholders at all levels to gain buy-in and ensure alignment.

b. Example: A healthcare provider conducts workshops with doctors, nurses, and administrators to gather input for its telemedicine platform.

13.5.1.3.   Adopt Agile Methodologies

a. Use Agile methodologies to enable iterative development and continuous improvement.

b. Example: A financial institution uses Agile to develop and deploy its mobile banking app in incremental releases.

13.5.1.4.   Invest in Skills Development

a. Provide training and upskilling opportunities to bridge skill gaps and empower employees.

b. Example: A logistics company offers IoT and data analytics training programs for its workforce.

13.5.2.   Real-Life Example

A financial institution successfully implemented a digital transformation initiative by starting with a clear vision, engaging stakeholders, adopting Agile methodologies, and investing in skills development. This approach resulted in improved customer satisfaction, reduced operational costs, and increased revenue.

13.6. Interactive Features and Exercises

To help readers engage with the content and apply the concepts, this chapter includes the following interactive elements:

13.6.1.1. Scenario-Based Exercise

a. Scenario: You are an IT Solutions Architect for a retail company planning a digital transformation initiative. The initiative includes adopting AI, IoT, and cloud computing to enhance customer experience and operational efficiency.

b. Task: Outline the key steps you would take to design and implement the solution. Consider strategic alignment, technology selection, and change management.

13.6.1.2. Reflection Prompt

a. Question: Think about a digital transformation initiative you've observed or been part of. What were the key challenges, and how were they addressed? What lessons can you apply to future projects?

13.6.1.3. Checklist for Digital Transformation

a. Define a clear vision and strategy aligned with business goals.

b. Engage stakeholders and gain buy-in for the initiative.

    c. Adopt Agile methodologies for iterative development and continuous improvement.

    d. Invest in skills development to bridge skill gaps and empower employees.

13.7. Real-World Case Studies

To provide deeper context, this chapter includes additional case studies from various industries:

13.7.1.1. *Finance*

A bank implemented a digital transformation initiative that included adopting cloud computing, AI-driven analytics, and a mobile banking app. The initiative improved customer satisfaction, reduced operational costs, and increased revenue.

13.7.1.2. *Healthcare*

A hospital adopted a telemedicine platform as part of its digital transformation strategy. The platform improved patient access to care, reduced wait times, and enhanced operational efficiency.

13.7.1.3. *Retail*

A retail company modernised its e-commerce platform by adopting AI-driven personalisation, IoT for inventory management, and cloud computing. The transformation resulted in increased sales, improved customer experience, and reduced operational costs.

13.8. Conclusion

Digital transformation is a complex but essential journey for organisations seeking to thrive in the digital age. IT Solutions Architects play a critical role in driving this transformation by aligning IT initiatives with business goals, selecting the right technologies, and navigating challenges. By following best practices and leveraging the right tools, IT Solutions Architects can deliver systems that provide long-term value. As you progress through this book, you'll gain the knowledge and tools needed to excel as an IT Solutions Architect.

Chapter 14: Career Development and Advancement

14.1. Introduction to Career Development and Advancement

Career development and advancement are essential for IT Solutions Architects who aim to grow professionally, take on leadership roles, and stay relevant in a rapidly evolving field. This chapter explores strategies for building a professional portfolio, continuous learning, and advancing to senior and leadership roles.

14.2. Building a Professional Portfolio and Network

A strong professional portfolio and network are critical for showcasing your expertise, gaining recognition, and opening doors to new opportunities. IT Solutions Architects must actively engage in activities that enhance their visibility and credibility.

14.2.1.   Key Strategies

14.2.1.1. Showcasing Projects

a.   Document your IT architecture projects, highlighting your role, challenges faced, solutions implemented, and outcomes achieved.

b.   Example: Create a portfolio website or LinkedIn profile that showcases case studies of your work, such as designing a scalable e-commerce platform or migrating a legacy system to the cloud.

14.2.1.2. Networking Events

a. Attend industry conferences, meetups, and networking events to connect with peers, mentors, and potential employers.

b. Example: Participate in events like AWS re:Invent, Microsoft Ignite, or local tech meetups to build relationships and stay informed about industry trends.

14.2.1.3. Online Presence

a. Maintain a professional online presence through platforms like LinkedIn, GitHub, or personal blogs to share insights, projects, and achievements.

b. Example: Regularly post articles on LinkedIn about your experiences with cloud architecture or contribute to open-source projects on GitHub.

14.2.2.   *Real-Life Example*

John, an aspiring IT Solutions Architect, regularly contributes to open-source projects on GitHub and shares his expertise on LinkedIn. His active engagement in online communities and participation in industry events help him build a strong professional network and gain recognition in the field. Over time, John's visibility leads to speaking opportunities at conferences and job offers from top tech companies.

14.3. Continuous Learning and Certification Paths

Continuous learning is essential for staying relevant and competitive in the ever-evolving field of IT Solutions Architecture. IT Solutions Architects must pursue certifications, specialised training, and stay updated with industry trends.

14.3.1. Key Learning Paths

14.3.1.1. Certification Programs

a. Pursue relevant certifications such as AWS Certified Solutions Architect, Microsoft Certified: Azure Solutions Architect, or Google Cloud Professional Architect to validate your expertise.

b. Example: Sarah, a seasoned IT Solutions Architect, completes the AWS Certified Solutions Architect certification to enhance her proficiency in cloud architecture.

14.3.1.2. Specialised Training

a. Enroll in online courses, boot camps, or workshops focused on specific technologies, methodologies, or domains relevant to IT architecture.

b. Example: Attend a workshop on serverless computing or container orchestration to broaden your skill set.

14.3.1.3. Industry Trends

a. Stay updated with the latest industry trends, best practices, and emerging technologies through blogs, webinars, podcasts, and industry publications.

    b. Example: Subscribe to newsletters like Gartner's IT Architecture Trends or follow thought leaders on LinkedIn to stay informed.

14.3.2.   Real-Life Example

Sarah, a seasoned IT Solutions Architect, completes the AWS Certified Solutions Architect certification to enhance her proficiency in cloud architecture. She also participates in specialised training programs on serverless computing and container orchestration to broaden her skill set and stay ahead of industry trends. This commitment to continuous learning helps her secure a promotion to a senior architect role.

14.4. Advancing to Senior and Leadership Roles in IT Architecture

Advancing to senior and leadership roles requires a combination of technical expertise, leadership skills, and business acumen. IT Solutions Architects must demonstrate leadership, align IT initiatives with business goals, and continuously improve their skills.

14.4.1. *Key Steps for Advancement*

14.4.1.1. *Demonstrating Leadership*

a. Take on leadership roles in projects, mentor junior team members, and contribute to strategic initiatives within your organisation.

b. Example: Lead a cross-functional team to design and implement a new enterprise architecture framework.

14.4.1.2. *Business Alignment*

a. Develop a deep understanding of business goals, challenges, and opportunities to align IT architecture initiatives with organisational objectives.

b. Example: Work closely with business stakeholders to design a data architecture that supports the company's analytics and decision-making needs.

14.4.1.3. *Continuous Improvement*

a. Seek feedback, reflect on past experiences, and proactively identify areas for improvement to continuously enhance your skills and capabilities.

b. Example: Conduct a retrospective after completing a major project to identify lessons learned and areas for growth.

14.4.2.   Real-Life Example

David, an experienced IT Solutions Architect, leverages his strong leadership skills and business acumen to transition into a senior leadership role. By championing innovative architectural solutions that drive business value and leading cross-functional teams, he earns recognition as a trusted advisor and strategic partner within his organisation. His ability to align IT initiatives with business goals leads to his promotion to Chief Technology Officer (CTO).

14.5. Interactive Features and Exercises

To help readers engage with the content and apply the concepts, this chapter includes the following interactive elements:

14.5.1.1.   Scenario-Based Exercise

a.   Scenario: You are an IT Solutions Architect aiming to advance to a senior leadership role. Your organisation is planning a major digital transformation initiative.

b.   Task: Outline the steps you would take to demonstrate leadership, align IT initiatives with business goals, and position yourself for advancement.

14.5.1.2. *Reflection Prompt*

a. Question: Think about your career journey so far. What steps have you taken to build your professional portfolio, expand your network, and pursue continuous learning? What areas would you like to focus on for future growth?

14.5.1.3. *Checklist for Career Development and Advancement*

a. Build a professional portfolio showcasing your projects and achievements.

b. Expand your network through online presence and networking events.

c. Pursue certifications and specialised training to enhance your skills.

d. Demonstrate leadership, align IT initiatives with business goals, and seek continuous improvement.

14.6. <u>Real-World Case Studies</u>

To provide deeper context, this chapter includes additional case studies from various industries:

14.6.1.1. *Finance*

A bank's IT Solutions Architect, Maria, pursued certifications in cloud architecture and data security. She also led a team to design a scalable, secure platform for online banking. Her efforts earned her a promotion to Head of IT Architecture.

14.6.1.2. Healthcare
A healthcare provider's IT Solutions Architect, Ahmed, attended industry conferences and specialised training in telemedicine technologies. He designed a telemedicine platform that improved patient access to care, leading to his promotion to Director of IT Solutions.

14.6.1.3. Retail
A retail company's IT Solutions Architect, Emily, built a strong online presence by sharing insights on LinkedIn and contributing to open-source projects. Her visibility led to speaking opportunities at industry events and a job offer as a Senior Solutions Architect at a leading tech firm.

14.7. Conclusion
Career development and advancement are essential for IT Solutions Architects who aim to grow professionally, take on leadership roles, and stay relevant in a rapidly evolving field. By building a strong professional portfolio, pursuing continuous learning, and demonstrating leadership, you can achieve your career goals and

make a lasting impact in the field of IT architecture. As you progress through this book, you'll gain the knowledge and tools needed to excel as an IT Solutions Architect.

Chapter 15: Conclusion: The Journey Ahead

15.1. Reflections on the Path to IT Solutions Architecture

Reflecting on your journey towards becoming an IT Solutions Architect is essential for personal growth and professional development. It allows you to acknowledge your achievements, learn from challenges, and identify areas for improvement.

15.1.1.   *Key Reflections*

15.1.1.1. *Milestones Achieved*

a. Acknowledge the milestones you've reached and the progress you've made in acquiring skills, knowledge, and experience in IT architecture.

b. Example: Completing certifications, leading successful projects, or mastering new technologies like cloud computing or microservices.

15.1.1.2. *Challenges Overcome*

a. Reflect on the challenges you've faced along the way and how you've overcome them through resilience, perseverance, and continuous learning.

b. Example: Transitioning from a technical role to an architectural role, managing complex stakeholder expectations, or navigating organisational resistance to change.

15.1.1.3. *Lessons Learned*

a. Identify key lessons learned from your experiences, projects, and interactions with peers and mentors that have shaped your growth as an IT architect.

b. Example: The importance of clear communication, the value of collaboration, or the need to balance technical depth with business acumen.

15.1.2.   *Real-Life Example*

Emily, a former business analyst, reflects on her transition to IT Solutions Architecture. Despite facing initial challenges in mastering technical concepts, she persevered through self-study, mentorship, and hands-on projects. Her reflections on the journey remind her of the valuable lessons learned and the growth achieved. For instance, she recalls how leading a complex cloud migration project taught her the importance of stakeholder engagement and risk management.

15.2. Future Outlook and Evolving Role of IT Architects

The role of IT Solutions Architects continues to evolve in response to technological advancements, industry trends, and changing business needs. Staying ahead of these changes is crucial for long-term success.

15.2.1.   *Key Factors Shaping the Future*

15.2.1.1. *Emerging Technologies*

a. Stay updated with emerging technologies such as artificial intelligence, machine learning, blockchain, and edge computing to anticipate future architectural requirements and opportunities.

b. Example: An IT Solutions Architect explores how quantum computing could revolutionise data encryption and optimisation problems.

15.2.1.2.   Agile and DevOps Practices

a. Embrace Agile methodologies and DevOps practices to enhance collaboration, agility, and innovation in IT architecture and project delivery.

b. Example: A Solutions Architect implements CI/CD pipelines to enable rapid and reliable deployment of new features.

15.2.1.3.   Business Strategy Alignment

a. Align IT architecture initiatives with broader business strategies and objectives to drive digital transformation, innovation, and competitive advantage.

b. Example: An IT Solutions Architect works closely with business leaders to design a data architecture that supports the company's analytics and decision-making needs.

15.2.2.   Real-Life Example

James, an experienced IT Solutions Architect, anticipates the future role of architects in driving digital transformation initiatives within organisations. By embracing Agile practices and fostering collaboration between development and operations teams, he envisions architects playing a pivotal role in accelerating innovation and delivering value to stakeholders. For instance, he leads a cross-functional team to design a serverless architecture that reduces costs and improves scalability.

15.3. Final Thoughts and Encouragement for Aspiring Architects

As you embark on your journey towards becoming an accomplished IT Solutions Architect, remember the following principles to guide your path:

15.3.1. Key Principles

15.3.1.1. Continuous Learning

a. Embrace a mindset of continuous learning, curiosity, and adaptability to stay relevant and thrive in a dynamic and rapidly changing IT landscape.

b. Example: Regularly attend industry conferences, pursue certifications, and explore new technologies to expand your skill set.

15.3.1.2. Resilience and Persistence

a. Expect challenges and setbacks along the way, but remain resilient and persistent in pursuing your goals and aspirations.

b. Example: Learn from failures, seek feedback, and use setbacks as opportunities for growth.

15.3.1.3. *Community and Support*

a. Seek support from peers, mentors, and communities within the IT industry to share knowledge, experiences, and insights and to navigate challenges together.

b. Example: Join professional networks like the Open Group or local tech meetups to connect with like-minded professionals.

15.3.2.   *Real-Life Example*

Sarah, a novice IT practitioner aspiring to become an IT Solutions Architect, finds inspiration and encouragement from the final thoughts shared by experienced architects in online forums and communities. Their words of wisdom remind her of the importance of resilience, continuous learning, and community support in achieving her career goals. For instance, she joins an online community where she receives mentorship and guidance on her journey.

15.4. Interactive Features and Exercises

To help readers engage with the content and apply the concepts, this chapter includes the following interactive elements:

15.4.1.1. *Reflection Exercise*

Task: Reflect on your journey so far. What milestones have you achieved? What challenges have you overcome? What lessons have you learned? Write a brief summary of your reflections.

15.4.1.2. *Future Planning Exercise*

Task: Identify three emerging technologies or trends that you want to explore further. Create a learning plan that includes courses, certifications, and hands-on projects to build your expertise in these areas.

15.4.1.3. *Community Engagement Exercise*

Task: Join an online community or professional network related to IT architecture. Participate in discussions, ask questions, and share your experiences to build connections and gain insights.

15.5. Real-World Case Studies

To provide deeper context, this chapter includes additional case studies from various industries:

15.5.1.1. Finance

A bank's IT Solutions Architect, Maria, reflects on her journey from a junior developer to a senior architect. She credits her success to continuous learning, resilience, and the support of her professional network. Maria now mentors aspiring architects and shares her experiences at industry conferences.

15.5.1.2. Healthcare

A hospital's IT Solutions Architect, Ahmed, shares how he overcame challenges in implementing a telemedicine platform. By embracing Agile practices and fostering collaboration, Ahmed successfully delivered a solution that improved patient access to care and earned recognition from senior leadership.

15.5.1.3. Retail

A retail company's IT Solutions Architect, Emily, reflects on her transition from a business analyst to an architect. She highlights the importance of continuous learning and community support in her journey. Emily now leads digital transformation initiatives that drive innovation and competitive advantage.

15.6. Conclusion

The journey to becoming an IT Solutions Architect is both challenging and rewarding. By reflecting on your achievements, embracing emerging trends, and staying committed to continuous learning, you can achieve your goals and make a lasting impact in the field. Remember to seek support from your community, remain resilient in the face of challenges, and align your work with the broader goals of your organisation. As you progress in your career, you'll find that the skills and experiences you gain will not only advance your professional growth but also contribute to the success of your organisation and the IT industry as a whole.

Additional Resources

- Cloud Academy: Architect Learning Paths (Becoming a Cloud Architect — Learn the Fundamentals | Cloud Academy)
- Microsoft Learn: Azure Architecture Center (Azure Architecture Center - Azure Architecture Center | Microsoft Learn)
- Google Cloud: Architecting with Google Cloud (Architecting with Google Compute Engine Specialization [5 courses] (Google Cloud) | Coursera)

About the Author

Olu Ogunsakin is a distinguished enterprise and solutions architect with over two decades of experience, specialising in cloud computing, enterprise architecture, and digital transformation. His illustrious career spans collaborations with Fortune 500 companies, government agencies, and leading financial institutions, where his strategic vision and meticulous approach to architecture design have consistently delivered tangible outcomes. Olu's expertise lies in optimising business processes, enhancing operational efficiency, and driving innovation through cutting-edge technological solutions.

Driven by a passion for knowledge-sharing and a desire to empower the next generation of IT professionals, Olu has embarked on a new chapter as a first-time author. His debut book, "Mastering IT Solutions Architecture: A Comprehensive Guide for Beginners and Practitioners," encapsulates years of practical experience, industry best practices, and actionable insights. This authoritative guide serves as a roadmap for navigating the complexities of IT solutions architecture, offering readers a comprehensive understanding of domain-driven design, cloud-based deployment models, Agile methodologies, and the software development lifecycle. Through real-world examples and practical advice, Olu equips aspiring and practicing architects with the tools and knowledge needed to excel in their careers.

Throughout his career, Olu has amassed an impressive portfolio of achievements and certifications, including:

- Certified Cloud Architect (AWS & Azure): Demonstrating unparalleled expertise in designing and implementing scalable, secure, and cost-effective cloud-based infrastructures.

- TOGAF® Certified: Mastery of The Open Group Architecture Framework (TOGAF) for developing enterprise architecture standards and practices that align with organisational goals.

- Agile and DevOps Practitioner: Proven ability to integrate Agile methodologies and DevOps practices into IT architecture, enabling faster delivery and continuous improvement.

Olu's contributions to the field extend beyond his professional achievements. As a mentor and thought leader, he is deeply committed to fostering talent and inspiring innovation within the IT community. His ability to simplify complex concepts and provide actionable guidance has made him a sought-after speaker at industry conferences and a trusted advisor to organisations worldwide.

In "Mastering IT Solutions Architecture," Olu combines his technical expertise with a passion for teaching, offering readers a unique

About The Author

blend of theoretical knowledge and practical application. His vision is to empower professionals and organisations to harness the full potential of technology, driving business success in an ever-evolving digital landscape.

Olu continues to lead and inspire in the dynamic world of enterprise and solutions architecture, embodying a commitment to excellence, innovation, and lifelong learning. As an author, mentor, and visionary, he remains dedicated to shaping the future of IT architecture and equipping professionals with the skills and confidence to thrive in their careers.

www.ingramcontent.com/pod-product-compliance
Lightning Source LLC
LaVergne TN
LVHW051338050326
832903LV00031B/3607